WHEN YOU GO TO TONGA

To "Ed" the "Ace" Missionary
with affection — Richard Keeling

WHEN YOU GO TO TONGA

By
Rev. Edward A. Tremblay, S.M.

With Preface by
His Eminence,
John F. Cardinal O'Hara, C.S.C., D.D.
Archbishop of Philadelphia

SECOND PRINTING

ST. PAUL EDITIONS

NIHIL OBSTAT:

> Michael Noonan, S.M.
> *Censor Deputatus*

IMPRIMI POTEST:

> James Lambert, S.M.
> *Provincial*

IMPRIMATUR:

> ✠ RICHARD CARDINAL CUSHING
> *Archbishop of Boston*

Library of Congress Catalog Card Number: 62-8918

Copyright, 1954, by the *Daughters of St. Paul*

Printed in U.S.A. by the *Daughters of St. Paul*
50 St. Paul's Ave., Jamaica Plain, Boston 30, Mass.

PREFACE

BY HIS EMINENCE,
JOHN F. CARDINAL O'HARA, C.S.C., D.D.
ARCHBISHOP OF PHILADELPHIA, PA.

Since the days of Captain Cook, tales of the sparkling islands of the South Pacific have had a fascination for readers, especially for those accustomed to long winter nights in the north countries of Europe and America. Explorers, geographers, botanists, poets, painters, and just plain story-tellers, have all tried their hand at giving the world a picture of the fairyland of the South Seas. And of course Hollywood has had its own versions.

But the real story of any place is the story of its souls. A new literature on the South Seas has come into being, and it is the work of missionaries, men and women. An artist can paint a sunset, a photographer can preserve the record of a typhoon, but only a soul endowed with supernatural grace can catch the beauty of another soul, can distinguish between an earthly and a heavenly paradise.

To the Society of Mary, a newly-founded religious congregation, the Holy See in 1836 entrusted the islands of western Oceanica. A few years later, in 1841, the blood of the first martyr, Blessed Peter Chanel, soaked the sands of Futuna, and the conquest for Christ began in earnest. Today the Vicariate of Wallis and Futuna, is completely Catholic; seven other Vicariates of the Marist Fathers extend westward to the Solomon Islands in the north and New Caledonia in the south, and carry the work of conversion and sanctification to hundreds of islands.

The American G.I.'s, in World War II, had ample reason to be grateful for the work of the missionaries, for the natives, many of them only two generations removed from cannibalism, bound the wounds and carried back to the American lines the service men whose planes or ships failed them in enemy territory. In the combat islands the G.I. was more aware of mosquitoes and swamps than of sandy beaches, but he learned to be grateful for the Christian virtues of the natives.

Father Tremblay, a Marist from New England, gives us bright glimpses of the soul of the Tongan, in this cheerful book. The spontaneous mirth of his stories reflects some of the hundredfold reward promised by our Divine Saviour to those who leave father and mother and all things for His sake. Each story reveals both the missionary and his charge, and some of the revelations are startling, for they show what God conceals from the proud and reveals to His simple children. Such, for example, is the story of Sister Mary Gabriel, the little Tongan girl whose vocation to be a Marist nun survived a cruel ordeal, and who thus explained why she chose her particular name in religion: "Patelé, when the Archangel Gabriel announced to the Blessed Virgin that she was to become the Mother of God, and when she said 'yes' and the Word became Flesh, that was the beginning of the Catholic Church, since it was the beginning of God made Man, wasn't it, Patelé?...I wanted St. Gabriel to be my special patron, so that I may become like another Gabriel for my people in Oua and by trying to be a good Sister, bring the beginning of the Catholic Church to the island where I was born."

This book deserves a wide reading, for it has the power to restore common sense and inspire love of God. And if it awakens some soul to a vocation, if it inspires the heroism needed for God's work in this world, it will be a blessed addition to the literature of the South Seas.

February 25, 1953

CONTENTS

CHAPTERS	PAGE
Preface	9
The Tears of St. Paul	21
The Kava Ring	33
Harvest Time in Tonga	41
Father Chevron's Last Diamond	51
Napoleon of the South Pacific	61
The Doctor Danced a Jig	76
The Boy Who Never Gave Up	84
The Hermit of Vavau	92
The Saint of Tin Can Island	100
One Fresh Egg for the Bishop	117
A Leper White as Snow	124
The Horse Didn't Genuflect	129
Bethlehem Comes to Tonga	136
A Joke on Father Thomas	148
Star of the Deep	153
The Big Brown Dog	158
He Threw a Book at His Mother-in-Law	164
Old Man Kerosene	172

CHAPTERS	PAGE
Esther and the Foolish Devil	181
Pango and the Shark	193
The Ghost Was Misbehavin'	202
God and Tonga Are My Heritage	206
Akapito's Thanksgiving	216
A Missionary's Simpler Pleasures	220
Sweet-Talking the Sharks	224
Something Special for Mother	230
He Dismantled a Mine With an Ax	238
The Cannibals Laughed Too	247
The Hula Dancer Who Became a Nun	254

Her Majesty the Queen of Tonga

THIS LITTLE BOOK

IS WRITTEN

IN HONOR

OF OUR LADY OF FATIMA,
THE QUEEN OF THE MOST HOLY ROSARY.

AND OF ST. PETER CHANEL, S.M.,

FIRST MARTYR OF OCEANIA.

AND IT IS

DEDICATED TO

HIS EMINENCE, RICHARD CARDINAL CUSHING,

ARCHBISHOP OF BOSTON,

FOR HIS GOD-INSPIRED

LOVE AND GENEROSITY FOR

THE MARIST MISSIONS

OF

OCEANIA.

ACKNOWLEDGEMENTS

The quotations from BISHOP SHANAHAN OF SOUTHERN NIGERIA, by John P. Jordan, C.S.Sp. are used with permission of the publishers, Clonmore & Reynolds Ltd., of Dublin, Ireland.

The poem TONGA, by the late J. Masterton, is reprinted with the permission of the Sidney (Australia) Bulletin in which it first appeared in 1913.

A ROYAL BIRTHDAY is reproduced by the courtesy of TIME, Copyright Time, Inc., 1950.

The photographs of Her Majesty, Queen Salote, are used with the permission of August Hettig, photographer in Nukualofa, Tongatapu.

A special tribute of gratitude from the author: —

1. To Mrs. Eileen Hall, a member of the Third Order of Mary in Atlanta, Ga., for her painstaking reading, expert editing and excellent typing of the manuscript. Mrs. Hall is editor of the book review page of THE BULLETIN of the Catholic Laymen's Association of Georgia and a former staff member of THE ATLANTA JOURNAL AND CONSTITUTION MAGAZINE.

2. To Joe Lane, of Chicago, Ill., staff cartoonist of EXTENSION MAGAZINE and author of MORE LITTLE NUNS, etc., for drawing for us, free of charge, the fine cartoons that illustrate several of our stories.

FOREWORD

LET'S GO TO TONGA.

"Where in the world is Tonga?" you ask, and that's just what we wanted you to ask.

The Kingdom of Tonga is 'way down in the romantic South Pacific, under the Southern Cross, nestled in the crooked elbow of the International Dateline, not many hundreds of miles from such other, better known islands as Samoa, Fiji and Tahiti.

To get to the Tongan Islands, you go from San Francisco to Honolulu. Then you sail southwest past Canton Island and, ten days later, on an ethereal moonlight night, you hear the magic cry of "Land ahead!" Ten miles away, right across the ship's bow, you see a long, dark-shadowed island. Its northern tip, which is more than 2000 feet high, reminds you of some peaceful supergiant, right out of Fairyland, quietly puffing away on his huge pipe.

Your Captain announces, "That is volcanic Tofua Island, on the western edge of the Haapai archipelago, the central part of the Kingdom of Tonga. By morning we reach Nukualofa, the capital, on the island of Tongatapu. Tomorrow at daybreak we pick up the pilot. An hour later we'll be alongside Nukualofa's wharf."

"Tofua," you muse aloud. And then you remember, "Oh, yes! 'The Mutiny on the Bounty'!"

And if you're up on Marist history, Nukualofa reminds you of Father Chevron, who offered the first Mass ever said in this part of the world, on a little island called Pangaimotu, within full sight of Tonga's capital city.

WHEN YOU GO TO TONGA you'll visit Father Chevron's grave, of course. And I wish you'd stop at the convent school in Nukualofa and visit Sister Mary Gabriel for me. In this book I've told you about both of them.

You may not have the regal good fortune of meeting Her Majesty, Queen Salote, who also lives in Nukualofa, and that's a pity, because she's a grand and gracious person. But maybe you'll visit His Excellency, Bishop John Rodgers, S.M., the Religious Superior, Father George Callet, S.M., and the other Marist Fathers, as well as the Marist Missionary Sisters, some of them Americans.

I'd especially like you to go to Houma which was my first "bush station" and where there is now a fine church and school. Quite different from the day there was "one fresh egg for the bishop." (We allude here to Bishop J. Blanc who is now very happily retired in Maufanga, Tongatapu.)

Anna Boyer and her mother, who used to live in this island, are now in New Zealand. I wish you could hear from them about the doctor who danced a jig. You won't see Tupou, the leper, either, because he's no longer in Tonga, but in the leper settlement in Makongai, Fiji. Too bad you can't meet that fine old man.

Maybe you'll take a long cruise through the Tongan Islands, as I did in 1924, and see for yourself the islands where our early Marists labored, even remote Tin Can Island, if you're hardy enough and willing to risk its tempestuous shores. You'll find Vavau more interesting after reading in this book the story of Father Breton, its saintly hermit, and knowing about the high hill (almost a mountain, in fact) there, where Blessed Peter Chanel planted a medal before he went on to Futuna and his martyrdom. In this same beautiful Vavau archipelago you'll visit the grave (yes, one grave for three priests) of Father Breton, Father Castagnier and Father Macé.

You'll stop in Lifuka, Haapai, (Father Peter Faone, S.M., is now in charge of Haapai,) of course, and chat with Father Herman Joseph Thérriault, the boy from Lille, Maine, who took over my post there, but is now in Niue Island starting a new mission in very great difficulties. He'll show you the beautiful church that was built because "the horse didn't genuflect" and the eager little boat we built and named "Star of the Deep" and many other things I've told you about in this book of stories. Old Man Kerosene has gone to his reward, but Pango is still there to tell you about his adventure with the shark. Oh, there are many people and places and things I want you to be sure and see WHEN YOU GO TO TONGA!

And who knows! You might fall in love with Tonga and decide to stay! Should this little book inspire even one missionary vocation for our Blessed Mother's cherished South Sea Island missions, we'll all thank God for making it an instrument of His will, like St. Paul's "vision in the night": — "That vision once seen, we were eager to sail. We concluded that God had called us there...."

CHAPTER 1

THE TEARS OF ST. PAUL

THIRTY YEARS are a long time when they represent what are generally considered the best years of a man's life.

Go back thirty years in your own life, if your memory reaches that far. All the years before that seem like a dream, don't they? Like a story you heard long ago about someone quite different from your present self.

How would it seem to be picked up, body and soul, out of your present existence, out of everything that spells LIFE to you now, today, and carried back, as if on a magic carpet — not to the same things and people and scenes and events of thirty years ago, but to the same place where those things were; to new things in the old familiar places; to new people and old friends who seem like new people, even though they share with you the old long-ago memories; to new scenes and new events springing from the same soil that nurtured those scenes and events that are now your memories of childhood and youth?

You can go back in space, but never in time.

I was not quite thirty years old — just two years a priest — when I left my native New England for Tonga, expecting to spend the rest of my life there. I was not quite sixty years old — more than half of those years in the priesthood — when I was again transplanted, this time from Tonga back to New England.

The first uprooting was hard; the second was something there is no word to express. Life in America, however much of it is left to me, in the wise designs of Providence, will never be the same as before I went away. My heart and the greater part of my soul are still in Tonga and will always be there. Nevertheless, it is God's will that the last part of my life, of my apostolate, should be another separate entity from the first two portions of it, and who knows but it may, after all, be the best part!

> "Grow old along with me,
> The best is yet to be," wrote Browning;
> "The last of life for which the first was made.
> Our times are in His hands
> Who saith, 'A whole I planned;
> Trust God, see all, nor be afraid.'"

God's secret designs for the future hold many surprises, no doubt. I look forward to them expectantly, even while Tonga never releases its hold upon me.

I miss my people. I miss many things that were part of my life those thirty years. One thing I miss very much is the sea. I think I must have spent ten of those thirty years at sea. I lived for twenty-five years right alongside the coralsand beach, within a few feet of the high-water mark. Beautiful coconut palms, huge banyan trees, more coconut trees, a few grass huts and wooden shacks, the stone church with its clock tower, the workshop and sawmill in my back yard, the refectory (a small building, about twenty feet from the rectory, which looked all the world like a chicken coop), the blue sea dotted with sails of native craft — such was my horizon all the way around. Here in Boston it's bricks and back alleys. But I'm getting used to it, for man is such an adaptable animal.

* * *

IMAGINE MY EMOTIONS when I recently read the following paragraphs in a book about another missionary, Bishop Joseph Shanahan, of Tipperary, Ireland, who also had spent exactly thirty years in the missions of Nigeria, Africa:

"When Bishop Shanahan retired.....life itself, as he understood it, came to an end. The human round of existence, with its hopes and projects, its efforts and achievements, its interests and appeals, was terminated. In Nigeria, there had been God and work, or more correctly God in work — the Divine and the human. Henceforth there was only God. There were memories of course ... and longings ... and heart-burnings ... and thoughts ... and feelings for the land and the people he loved. But these were lost in God, and seen in Him and felt in Him. Even the land of Africa was caught up in the greater love of God.

"'You ask me,' he said, 'what is the lure of the missions, the fascination that always seems to be calling to the missionary to return? As well ask St. Paul to explain the tears that flowed down his bearded cheeks on the strand at Miletus, when his newly converted Christians gathered around him to bid a last goodbye. Such things are always a mystery to the man who has not experienced them. But once a man has tasted God, the experience takes the savour from all other joys. When he has lived in the midst of life, of the Life of God in the souls of men as rich and luxuriant and fruitful as the life of prodigal Nature in these tropics — above all, when that man has been the vessel chosen by God for His scattering of this exuberant Life, and been given a grace of paternity deeper and closer than what is merely human — that man, I say, would be less than human if his heart-strings did not pull him almost irresistibly back to where the title of Father has most meaning for him.'"

Bishop Shanahan had gone back to Ireland on account of ill health. The story of his life continues: "He realized.....that retirement was for him both a purification of his sensitive nature and a preparation for eternity. But there was nothing self-centred about this preparation. 'God has shown me that my few little activities are to consist in getting back to the strict practice of Community life, and that means to a life of prayer. In His goodness, God has given me ample time to pray. And prayer means apostolate, apostolate in Nigeria. By prayer, the offering of the Holy Sacrifice, the acceptance of whatever crosses life in its last lap holds in store for me, I continue to be a missionary even in Ireland.'"

NOW YOU KNOW why I have written this book of stories about Tonga, true stories of many of the highlights of those thirty "best years of my life." Like the Irish Bishop, thanks be to God, I continue to be a missionary — even in America!

* * *

IN 1913, EIGHT YEARS before I ever saw Tonga, an Englishman who later became a good friend of mine, wrote some picturesque verses about the little island kingdom, showing how he too had fallen in love with his adopted land. "But when we come to part," he concluded, "There's something in you, Tonga, that keeps tugging at my heart."

The late J. Masterton was at one time vice British Consul in Nukualofa, the capital of Tonga. Some of the references mentioned in his amusing little tribute to the island kingdom are no longer true, forty years later, but one thing certainly remains the same. Tonga is a place blessed by Almighty God with a peace and prosperity that can be found hardly anywhere else in the world.

Mr. Masterton's poem, entitled "Tonga," reads:

O have you heard of Tonga, a funny little place?
A king rules there in purple by Britain's saving grace,
With ministers and nobles and parliaments that meet
Triennially only ... and then just meet to eat.

O have you heard of Tonga, that lone Pacific realm,
Those lingering, last islands with brown men at the helm?
Some coral heaps and atolls, some bits of palm-fringed beach,
Where squat some tired "apostles" who live to sing and preach.

That's all there is of Tonga. Not much to write about;
Not much to make exploiters or tourists rave and spout.
Therein lies its salvation. By reason of its great,
Its regal unimportance, it rests a native state,

A bit anachronistic, as wags the world today
But pretty as a picture, funny as a play.
With olden rules fast changing and giving place to new,
Stagnation's a refreshing and novel thing to view;
And nowhere is stagnation more wholly at its best
Than just in "Holy Tonga's" division of the blest.

A land of peace and plenty; a group of goody goods...
In precept ... though in practice it has its naughty moods.
A race the cognoscente, with justice claim to be
By far the best off people in this quaint Southern Sea.

Some visitors grow carping. They judge the place asleep.
They say it's so untidy it makes the angels weep.
But Heaven holds no judgment for aught the Tongans do;
They long ago annexed it and all its "angels" too.

You're narrow, little Tonga; you're what the Scots call "blate,"
Your only book's the Bible, which isn't up to date.
You've no chance to learn things; but don't know what you miss,
And ignorance in your case I fain to think spells bliss.

Wrapped up in self-contentment, you dream from day to day.
You don't know what you're here for. (Do we know anyway?)
You only see you're living; you feel the earth is fair;
You've found a satisfaction we can't find anywhere.

O happy, lazy Tonga, you tiny useless land!
There's neither fame nor fortune to harvest from your strand.
I know you breed unfitness, but when we come to part,
There's something in you, Tonga, that keeps tugging at my heart.

* * *

TONGA HAS PROGRESSED in many ways since 1913. Since World War II especially, the people have become more appreciative of education, more aware of the world beyond their island home. Their parliament now meets once each year, instead of "triennially only."

The king who reigned "in purple, by Britain's saving grace," King George Tupou II of Tonga, died in 1918 and was succeeded by his 18-year-old daughter, Salote Tupou. "Queen Salote's name, the Tongan equivalent of Charlotte, was given her in honor of her great-great-grandmother who, in turn, was named after Charlotte of Mecklenburg, Consort of Britain's George III," explained an article in the March 27, 1950 issue of TIME magazine, on the occasion of Queen Salote's fiftieth birthday, which had been celebrated on March 13.

The TIME article, entitled "A Royal Birthday," quoted from Captain James Cook's "Voyages": 'Both men and women are of a common size with

Europeans... The women ... were the merriest creatures... and kept chattering without the least invitation..."

(They haven't changed much since, have they?)

"... They are seldom disturbed by either foreign or domestic troubles (and) appeared healthy, strong and vigorous — a proof of the goodness of the climate in which they live."

The TIME article continued: "Last week, 177 years after Captain Cook's ships dropped anchor there, the tall, brown people of Tonga, still strong and vigorous, were enthusiastically celebrating a royal birthday: Salote, the strapping (6 ft. 2 in.) Queen of the Tongans and a Dame Commander of the British Empire, was 50 years old.

"Tongans could celebrate Queen Salote's birthday with good reason. In her 32 years' reign, Salote has capably and efficiently continued the tradition of a peaceful Polynesian dynasty that has ruled Tonga's 150 islands (total area: 250 sq. miles; pop. 45,000) for almost 3½ centuries. Tongans have no housing problem, no unemployment; they get free medical and dental care. Education (including English, Tongan history, singing and native arts) is compulsory from the age of six to 14.

"Debt & Taxes. Under Queen Salote's diligent administration, Tonga has built up sizable overseas investments. The islands, which became a

British protectorate in 1900, have no income tax, no public debt and a remarkably low crime rate: one murder in 30 years. At the age of 16, every male Tongan gets eight acres of land, for which he pays an annual tax of about $7 U. S. to the Tongan government and a token rental to his chief. Tonga has its own passports, its own currency and its own postal system (including the station, famed among philatelists, of 'Tin Can Island').

"In the last 50 years, Tonga has experienced only two real crises, one minor and one major. The minor crisis was World War II (Tonga formally declared war on Germany in September 1939, with a proclamation that began: 'We, Salote...')."

(There was, at the time, only one machine gun in the kingdom and ammunition for only one minute.)

"In the spring of 1942, U. S. troops went ashore on Tonga with orders to 'take the island and destroy the enemy.' The invaders were met by a group of friendly Tongans who explained that they had heard of Pearl Harbor long before, had promptly tossed all of the islands' 100-odd Japanese into jail in the capital city of Nukualofa. Later, thousands of other Allied soldiers stopped off at the Tongan Islands on their way to & from the Pacific battlefronts. During this time, Queen Salote wisely instructed her people to retire to the interior, safely avoided any entanglements, economic or romantic, between the Tongans and the GIs.

"Cricket & Crisis. Tonga's major crisis occurred at the turn of the century, when the British introduced cricket to the islands. The Tongans were so fascinated with the game that they abandoned their work en masse. Even toddlers and old men insisted on playing, while the copra mildewed on the ground and the pigs ate the overripe bananas. A special meeting of the Tongan cabinet was called to meet the crisis and the cabinet decided to ask the British consul for advice. The consul suggested that the Tongan Assembly pass a law limiting the playing of cricket to two days a week. The cabinet took his advice, the law is still on the books, and the Tongans have lived happily ever after."

* * *

WHEN FATHER PETER CHANEL (who later was killed by the inhabitants of Futuna and thus became the first Marist martyr; and was canonized in 1954) came to Tonga in October, 1837, he immediately fell in love with those black-eyed, intelligent brown people. He admired their clean, cool, oval-shaped houses, built of native wood and coconut leaves. Meals were prepared in a sort of fireless cooker and served on breadfruit leaves. No need for any dish-washing. There was plenty of food everywhere.

The beds were mats spread on the floor; the pillow a rounded-off block of wood. Tapa, a paper-like fabric, and very warm, served as blankets. The natives were keen to learn. How Father Chanel would have loved to stay! The king would gladly have accepted him but, influenced by an impious white man, he was obliged to send the priest away. Before he left, however, Father Chanel climbed to the top of the highest hill in the Vavau archipelago and buried a medal of the Blessed Virgin in the soil, fervently praying for the Kingdom of Tonga.

Should you ever go to Vavau and enter its beautiful harbor, one of the most fascinating in the South Seas, a tall, dignified native priest will greet you and show you around the Catholic Mission. He is Father Gregory Kailao, S.M., now in his middle fifties. Not only is he the successful pastor of the entire Vavau archipelago, but he is also a great builder and a good business man. You would be surprised to see the beautiful concrete church Father Gregory designed and paid for, with only the help of his fellow natives.

Father Gregory was born at the foot of the high hill where St. Peter Chanel planted that medal of the Blessed Virgin — just a few hundred miles from Futuna where the martyr died.

The blood of marytrs is always and forever the seed of the Church — and of the priesthood too!

CHAPTER 2

THE KAVA RING

IT WAS OCTOBER 2, 1921, Feast of the Holy Angels, a beautiful day of entrancing calm and sunshine. We were slowly steaming past a little green island called Atata, which stands sentinel-like near one of the two passes leading into the waters of Tongatapu. We were day-dreaming over the huge, rust-eaten wreck of a once beautiful American steamer, when a good New Zealand Irishman tapped me on the shoulder and, pointing to a long, low, palm-fronded island stretching crescent-wise on the horizon, said with an Irish twinkle in his eye, "That's Tongatapu, Father. There's your island waiting for you."

My island!

Did you ever think of how a young missionary must feel when, after the ever unforgettable parting from all that is near and dear to him in this world, after the long, long voyage to the field afar, he first sees his "promised land," the strange, new home God has given him to evangelize, to live and perhaps to die in?

My island! Tongatapu! Feast of the Holy Angels, 1921!

As the line of red-roofed houses that marked the capital of Tonga grew in definiteness, and the Queen's Palace with its stone-walled compound, the large, well kept government buildings and the long concrete wharf became visible, all the previous ideas I'd had of Tonga came tumbling down like a castle of dominoes.

An hour later we were alongside Nukualofa's wharf. Long before we left the ship we could clearly distinguish the cassocks of the two Marist Fathers who had come to meet their new young assistant. With their long beards and ascetic faces one might have mistaken them for St. Joseph and St. Francis de Sales in person. But no, the jolly little old Frenchman with a twinkle of mischief in his eye and the St. Joseph beard was Father Emelien Thomas, S.M., pastor of Maufanga. I was to be his assistant for the next few years. The other confrere, who looked for all the world like St. Francis de Sales, always smiling and ever on the lookout to make someone happy, was Father Albert Kerrman, S.M., who had arrived just the year before and was in charge of Vavau archipelago.

"Here's the carriage waiting for you," said Father Thomas with a smile of paternal pride. Sure enough, there was an old-time rig hitched to a bay horse that was standing on three legs and sleeping with one eye half open.

We were off for Maufanga, Father Thomas' large parish, almost two miles from Nukualofa, the capital of the Kingdom. Father Thomas was 63 years old then, and wonderfully active still, after 37 years of missionary life in Tonga. He was our second oldest Father and, like all old missionaries, loved to speak of days gone by.

He was a witty story-teller. One tale that he particularly liked to tell over and over again (without remembering he had just told it the day before, God bless him!) was the story of Brother John and the little pig.

"I had just arrived in Tonga," he would begin. "Of course they wished to celebrate the coming of a new missionary in the Tongan way, and that meant that at least one pig had seen its last day. The stout, philosophical Brother John, whose long years spent in the missions (and his long beard too) made one think of the patriarchs of old, happened to be cook at that time.

"After much puffing and sweating, Brother John had managed to get hold of a most unwilling little grunter. 'Please, Father,' he said, 'hold him for me till I fetch the knife.' I was quite amused.

This was a new experience for me, just out of the seminary in Rome. I was beginning to feel quite proud of my ability at holding a pig when, all of a sudden, the wiggling little fellow, spying old Brother John coming along with a big, long knife in his hand, slipped out of my hands and made a dash for freedom to the nearby forest.

"Brother John was dumbfounded. 'Did ye ever see the likes of it?' he gasped under his breath. And then, after a solemn pause, he added with a wise shake of the head, 'Father, 'tis all very well to be learned and to be a Roman Doctor, but I see you don't know how to hold a pig!'"

Father Thomas was the author of the Lives of the Saints in Tongan and the founder of our Catholic College of Api Foou in Maufanga. He died in Lapaha, Tongatapu, on June 27, 1942, after suffering for many years with asthma.

We rode along toward Maufanga, behind the sleepy bay horse, on that feast of the Holy Angels in 1921. Soon, through the coconut groves and over the brown roofs and the weed-and-leaf-built Tongan huts, we saw the large, low church with its gable roof and bell tower in the rear.

"It's our cathedral," Father Thomas informed me, "and Benediction of the Blessed Sacrament is just over. Do you recognize the Father you see over there in the kava ring with all the Tongan catechists and other Catholics around him?"

Did I! How a beard does change a man! Yet there was no doubt about it! It was Father Elias Bergeron, the first American Marist in Oceania, another native of the great Archdiocese of Boston. Father Bergeron, with his thick black beard, looked much different from when I had last seen him some eight or ten years before, when he was our English professor at Marist Seminary in Washington, D. C.

Like the father of the prodigal son, he spied me from afar and, running forth to greet me, fell on my neck, and I fell on his beard, getting my glasses caught and nearly breaking his with the thick rim of the helmet I had forgotten to take off.

This was the hit of the day for our keen-eyed Tongans. They were bubbling over with delight as "Patele Elia" (Father Bergeron's Tongan name) escorted the "prodigal son" to their kava meeting. "Malo e folau leleimai!" (Congratulations on your happy voyage!) they cried. Of course I could answer only by broadside smiles and deaf-and-dumb signals.

I will always remember that first kava-making that I attended in Tongatapu. How happy everyone looked! All knew the great need of priests and, now that Divine Providence had sent them another, they were joyously grateful. America had heard the call of unknown Oceania. American Marist priests were coming, in all confidence and humility, to supplement their brothers from Europe who had labored there since 1842, when Father Joseph Chevron, S.M., a 34-year-old French Marist, said the first Mass in Tonga on the Feast of Our Lady's Visitation.

But that's another story. Now I want to tell you about my first drink of kava. "What's kava?" you're wondering. It's a drink made from the root of a shrub named the "piper methysticum." In more primitive days it was prepared by chewing. Now stones are used. After the root is well pounded, water is poured over it. The mixture becomes mustard color. More water is added and the concoction is strained through a fiber strainer and served from coconut shells.

It is presented to the various members of the kava ring in the order of their rank and importance, the third bowl generally going to the biggest chief present. Why doesn't he get the first one? Because, according to a custom that originated long years ago, two other prominent men must drink before he does to prove that no attempt is being made to poison the big chief. Each one's name is called and he answers by clapping his hands. It is considered impolite not to drain the shell at one draught.

I'd had my first experience with the native drink a short time earlier when we passed through American Samoa on the way to Tonga. Father John Dumas, S.M., was the resident priest at the Pago Pago church then.

"You won't be able to drink a mouthful," he kept telling me as we watched the kava-making ceremonies.

Two natives, wearing something around their waists that looked like fine straw mats, squatted before us and one of them placed a piece of old, whitish root at my feet. "That's kava," Father Dumas whispered. "Touch it." I took the old thing up and felt very much like whittling it to see what it looked like inside. In the Samoan etiquette (and Tongan too) that would have been a terrible thing to do — almost a sacrilege.

Then the man who had brought the kava began to make a speech. Father Dumas translated, as the orator continued thanking God "to have brought over from America another Father who is going to spend his life in the poor little unknown islands of Oceania." The strange language had a beautiful sound and the good man's face was aglow with sincerity and gratitude. I had to say a few words in reply, and Father Dumas translated them, and by that time our kava was nearly ready.

A girl had been preparing it for the last fifteen minutes. Placing the kava root on a round, black stone, she had been pounding it with a smaller one until the root was reduced to yellowish pulp. She put this pulp into a large wooden bowl called "kumete" and poured water into it until the whole mass became semi-liquid and mustard color. Then more water was poured in and she proceeded to strain the whole thing through a fiber strainer called "fau." She would gather all the solid matter in the "fau" and wring it as dry as she could. During the whole operation her hands were wrist-deep in the kava bowl. But they were clean — at least when she got through the wringing.

Father Dumas was still smiling and warning me of the unusual taste. I made up my mind to drain the whole cup, no matter what it tasted like. The coconut cup was presented with the usual graceful bow, the palm of the bearer's hand being lifted and turned upward.

As calmly as if it had been a cup of tea, I started to drink. My, what a taste! In appearance it's like yellow-tinted dishwater, and its taste is so strange and so different from anything one ever drank before that it's impossible to know what to compare it with. Old tea, mustard, carbolic acid, soap, castor oil — all these passed through my imagination as I was introduced to the sacred beverage.

Let me hasten to add, however, with all due respect to the national drink of Oceania, that in reality it's a blessing and its making is the occasion of much good for the missionary. Nothing is so cooling and refreshing in the tropical climates as a good bowl of kava. One soon gets used to the taste and neither Sunday Mass nor any other occasion is complete without its kava party.

CHAPTER 3

HARVEST TIME IN TONGA

FATHER BERGERON, our first American Marist in Oceania, was in charge of the Catholic College for Boys in Maufanga when I arrived there in 1921. His assistant was Father Emile Leniel, S.M., a French priest. The College (called Api Foou) is about four minutes' walk from the Maufanga Mission. It then consisted of a group of low, wooden buildings and Tongan houses and a graceful, octagonal-shaped coral chapel situated in the midst of picturesque ironwood trees and palm-fronded coconuts.

After serving from 1935 to 1947 as Provincial of Oceania, Father Bergeron is now pastor in a nice little nook of Fiji — Levuka, Ovalau. Father John Rodgers, S.M., from New Zealand, is in charge of the college and running it on the proverbial shoestring, with only native tutors. He has about 380 students. He is doing a wonderful job. He has also built a fine new College Chapel.

The College was founded in the eighteen-nineties by Father Thomas, who was young and strong then, full of youthful energy and zeal. It has played an important role in the growth and development of the Tongan Mission. It has trained our catechists, our schoolmasters and produced a class of well bred, well trained Catholics who are the joy and consolation of the heroic Fathers who have spent themselves unstintingly in this often tedious and ungrateful task.

Father Bergeron's long experience in college work in America, his knowledge of boys and the wonderful authority he had over them had prepared him well for the job. From the beginning of his taking charge, his work there was crowned with consoling success.

It was no easy task to manage seventy or eighty Tongan lads and make them do something they had never done before coming to college — work! I couldn't help noticing with wonder and admiration the truly remarkable discipline which prevailed. Our American boys would be ashamed of themselves if they could see the good conduct, good spirit and dutifulness of many of those Tongan lads.

How do they pay for their education? What do they learn? What do they eat? They pay nothing. Tuition and board are entirely free. They earn these by their work. Three days of each week are school days; the other three are devoted to manual labor. On these working days, the boys go out, under the care of a devoted helper, and work at their plantations of yams, taros, kumalas, etc. They return to the school ready to resume their studies under their beloved professors.

When yams are plentiful the college menu consists of yams for breakfast, yams for dinner, yams for supper, with a banana or "ifi" (Tongan chestnut) thrown in for flavor. They never tire of yams, just as we in America never tire of bread. When the yams give out they eat "kumalas" (sweet potatoes) and other native food. On "big days" the main dish is a "puaka" (pig).

All these are cooked in primitive "fireless cookers." Here's how it's done. A few stones are placed in a freshly dug hole. A fire is made over them and then raked away, leaving only the red hot stones. These are covered over with leaves and soil. The food to be cooked is wrapped in leaves and placed on top. More leaves are added to give the right flavor, and finally all is covered over with a grave-like mound of dirt. When meal time comes, two or three hours later, out of the fireless cooker comes a perfectly well done pig or chicken and a steaming pile of native vegetables.

The Tongans sit on the floor of their houses to eat. The floor is made of plaited coconut leaves and another plaited palm frond is spread on the floor in the middle of the group of people. This is the table. The big roast pig, its insides filled with sweet smelling herbs, is in the center. At regular intervals along the table are little bags made from banana leaves. These contain banana soup.

Spoons? A Tongan cuts off a small piece of a banana leaf, folds it in a certain way and, behold, there's the tropical island spoon ready for action. There are no other knives and forks than one's fingers. There is no salt or pepper. The natives wonder why and how white people talk while they eat. They themselves remain silent for the simple reason that they can't talk because their mouths are chock-full all during the meal.

All this is true of the college boys, as of all the other natives. Now what do they learn at the college? First of all, the program aims to give them a thorough knowledge of the Catholic religion, from both the theoretical and the practical points of view. Each boy is taught to serve Mass. The Tongan lads love to do this and they serve in a most edifying way. They are taught Tongan and English, arithmetic, geography and history. English is quite difficult for them. It's so different from their native tongue, yet they're most willing to learn. Their own alphabet has only sixteen letters and all Tongan words end with a vowel sound. Naturally English confuses them.

There's a girls' school in Maufanga too. It is situated close to the beautiful coral church and is under the motherly care of the Marist Missionary Sisters. In 1921, when I arrived there, the Superior of the girls' school was a veteran French missionary nun whom everyone called "Mamé." Everybody in Tonga knew Mamé, whose real name was Sister Mary Xavier. Both Catholics and non-Catholics had the deepest love and veneration for her. She was then 67 years old and had been in Tonga 42 years, since leaving her work in one of the best hospitals of Lyons, France, to come to the missions.

Father Bergeron introduced me to her on the day of my arrival. When I saw that venerable, weather-beaten countenance, where even the wrinkles seemed to smile, those once delicate hands now hardened and worn by hard work, those kind motherly eyes so full of the peace and joy that the true missionary knows, I thought of a beautiful poem I once knew about a Sister of Charity. Here before me was its living realization.

> She once was a lady of honor and wealth,
> Bright glowed on her features the roses of health,
> Her vesture was blended of silk and of gold,
> And her motion shook perfume from every fold....

> She felt in her spirit the summons of grace,
> That called her to live for the suffering race;
> And heedless of pleasure, of comfort, of home,
> Rose quickly like Mary, and answered, "I come."

Mamé, died in 1923. During the long illness that terminated in her beautiful death, she was visited by Her Majesty, Queen Salote, who embraced her repeatedly, thanking her in the name of the Royal Family for all she had done for Tonga in her long and fruitful life. Her funeral was one of the most impressive ever seen in the little kingdom. Now Mamé rests in her little Tongan grave of white sand, while the memory of her hidden life of humility and charity remains one of the unique glories of the Catholic Church in Tonga.

The girls' school has since been enlarged, but it is still staffed by the Marist Missionary Sisters, who have a novitiate there for native Sisters.

Maufanga, on the north coast of Tongatapu, near Nukualofa, the capital, is one of the two main centers of the Catholic Mission there. The other is Mua, on the south and east, the most flourishing district on the island, with its great Catholic town of Lapaha, and six outlying villages. The third and last district, the smallest and poorest of the three, is Hihifo, or Western Tonga.

Tongatapu itself is one of three principal groups of islands that make up the Kingdom of

Tonga, the one remaining nominally independent state of the Pacific. The others are the Haapai group and the Vavau group, each separated from the others by several hours' sail. Far to the north are two islands, Niua Toputapu (Keppels Island) and Niua Foou (Tin Can Island), which also come under the Tongan government, though separated from the main groups by several hundred miles.

Most all the islands are of coral, with a covering of soil, but all were raised from the sea by volcanic action. The soil is a rich clay loam of an average depth of from twelve to fifteen feet. The Tongatapu and Haapai groups are typical South Sea islands, low-lying, with the coconut predominant everywhere. The Vavau group was thrown up higher from the sea and has some hills with rugged outlines. There are no streams in the kingdom, except in Eua Island where most of the former inhabitants of Tin Can Island have taken refuge since the volcano there erupted in 1942. Rain water is used for drinking and cooking.

Before World War I, fourteen Marist Fathers were laboring in Tonga. When I arrived in 1921, there were only nine: His Excellency, Bishop Joseph Blanc, S.M., D.D., in Maufanga and Nukualofa; Father Thomas, Father Bergeron, Father Leneil and Father Kermann; Father Francis Deguerry, S.M., of Lapaha; Father John Baptiste Mace,

S.M., in charge of the Haapai archipelago and Keppels; Father Peter Jouny, S.M., and his native assistant, Father Petelo Liku, S.M., in Niua Foou.

It was harvest time in Tonga — time to reap what our predecessors had sown in their lifelong martyrdom of charity. The harvest was indeed great and the laborers were few — pitifully few. They still are.

For instance, there is an unfortunate situation in the isolated Keppels group, 165 long sea miles to the north of Vavau and 300 miles from Nukualofa. Father Peter Wall, S.M., of New Zealand, is now in charge of this remote Mission. Whenever he leaves for a trip to Tongatapu he must consume the Sacred Species and, for two, three or sometimes more months, the Sisters at Keppels have to undergo their hardest privation of all — no Holy Mass, no Holy Communion, no Blessed Sacrament in their empty Tabernacle. Missionaries know privation of many sorts, but this is by far the worst kind.

This situation is due in part to the fact that since World War II a policy of restriction on non-native ministers of religion is in effect. This permits only the status quo of the number of white ministers of religion and, strangely, Sisters and Brothers are included in this exclusion policy. To be allowed more than this, any denomination must have an increase of 2000 members for each new minister of religion. Let us pray the Lord of the harvest to enlighten those who created this policy, so they will understand all its tragic implications, such as the sad state of affairs in Keppels.

In 1921 there were about 3000 Catholics in Tonga's total population of about 23,000. Both the population and the number of Catholics have just about doubled since then. There were nine Marist priests (one a native), three native diocesan priests, and thirty Marist Missionary Sisters, about half of them native, working in the Kingdom of Tonga in 1951, when my superiors brought me back to America to tell my countrymen about Mary's little-known lands of the South Pacific.

Of the fourteen Marist Fathers who were my confreres thirty years ago, His Excellency, Bishop Blanc, is the only one still remaining in Tonga. Father Bergeron is in Fiji. Father Deguerry is pastor of Our Lady of Victories, Lester Square, in London. The others have finished their work on earth but, like St. Therese, Patroness of the Missions, they are "spending their heaven" continuing the good work that was their God-given task on earth.

Those who have replaced them are: Father Paul Boussit, S.M., who is pastor on Eua Island (across the "Tongan Deep" from Tongatapu) and still Vicar General of the Vicariate of Tonga; Religious Superior, Father G. Callet, S.M., and Father Petelo Maka are in charge of the Hihifo district of

Tongatapu; Father Leo Roy, S.M., and Father C. Butler, S.M., are in charge of the Mua district; Father Edward Schahl, S.M., and Father Felise Napole are in charge of the Maufanga or central district of Tongatapu. Father Peter Faone is in charge of the Haapai Archipelago; Father Gregory Kailao in charge of Vavau Archipelago; Father Peter Wall in charge of Keppels Island. Father J. Thérriault is actually founding a new mission on Niue Island. And of course—last but not least—the new Bishop of Tonga, His Excellency, Bishop John Rodgers is still in charge of our College of Apifoou near Nukualofa!

CHAPTER 4

FATHER CHEVRON'S LAST DIAMOND

IN OUR PARISH of Maufanga, in the early nineteen-twenties, there was an old, old woman, named Losa (Rosa), who still remembered the arrival of the first Marists in Tongatapu. I heard her tell in her simple vivid way how she, as a small child, followed Bishop Pompallier and his party from the shore to the King's palace where she saw and heard all that took place in their history-making interview.

It was July 1, 1842 when the Marists came — July first, eve of Our Lady's Visitation — July first, later named the Feast of the Most Precious Blood of Jesus — July first, just a little more than a year after the first Marist martyr's blood hallowed the soil of neighboring Futuna Island and, as martyrs' blood has done since the first Good Friday, became the seed from which the Church eternally springs. Blessed Peter Chanel had won his martyr's crown just fourteen months earlier, on April 28, 1841.

The coming of a ship is even today a great event in the islands, so when the "Sancta Maria" appeared on the dark blue brim of Tongatapu's horizon you may be sure the keen-eyed natives watched it with the greatest interest, little dreaming that it was bringing them the founders of the Catholic Church in Tonga — Bishop John Baptiste Pompallier, Father Joseph Chevron, S.M., Brother Attale, S.M., the newly converted king of nearby Wallis Island and a large party of other Catholics.

Like a huge white bird gradually alighting after a long flight, the ship lowered its sails and cast anchor off Pangaimotu, a snug little island in full view of Nukualofa. The next morning the first Mass ever said in this part of the world was offered by Father Chevron on a rustic altar set up beneath a huge banyan tree on the little island. A fresh breeze, like the rustling of angels' wings, murmured gently through the great banyan's forest of foliage; then, like a child at play, joyously rippled the blue-green waters of Pangaimotu Bay and fled off invisibly to frolic with the palm-fronded island of Tongatapu. Everything was wrapped in the fresh, joy-thrilling calm of morning. All nature, on that beautiful Visitation Day, must surely have thrilled with rapture under the Master's Feet during this, the first Sacrifice of the Mass ever offered in this tiny corner of the world that He came and died to save.

"Glory be to God in the highest....and peace to men of good will!.... Come, ye gentiles, to adore the Lord: for this day a great light hath descended. Sing joyfully to God, all the earth: make melody and rejoice and sing."

During that Holy Mass, how the young missionary must have gazed lovingly at the island where God was calling him, where he would spend all the rest of his long life; how he must have offered up beforehand all those long years of hard toil, his sacrifices and prayers, his hours of joy and sorrow, and even his life should it please God to let him die for His Love's sake as his friend, Father Chanel, had been privileged to die just the year before.

Father Chevron was born in 1808 in the quaint old town of Nantua, France. In 1829, a year before his ordination to the priesthood, he confided to his Bishop, Monsignor Alexander Raymond Devie, of Lyons, his desire to be a missionary. "Where do you intend to go?" the Bishop asked. "What missionary society do you feel inclined to join?" In his sincere longing and candid love for the missions, young Joseph Chevron had simply never thought of those details. So Bishop Devie told him, "Young man, reflect more over this matter, and pray.....and remind me of it ten years hence."

Ten years! For a young, zealous heart that seemed like a century. But it was God's Holy Will. In later years Father Chevron used to remind his fellow-missioners of that providential delay. "For then," he would add, "the Society of Mary had not yet been given the Oceanian missions."

After his ordination he was sent as professor to the seminary at Belley, where he met Father Jean Claude Colin, founder of the newly formed little Society of Mary, and his first companions. The extreme poverty of the bare, cold attic room in which the little community lived; their simple, quiet, joyful way; their profound humility and piety; and most of all the name of the infant Society, won Father Chevron's heart. In 1839, exactly ten years after his first appeal to Bishop Devie, he received all the necessary permissions to join the Society of Mary and to go to Oceania.

The parting with his beloved mother was difficult, as such partings always are for missionaries. But as mothers usually do, she encouraged him: "You are a priest, my son. You are a priest, and who am I to oppose the rights of God? Go where He calls you — only promise me I will see you again."

"Yes, Mother, we shall see each other again," he promised, and then added in a whisper, "but only in Heaven!"

From London, aboard the Australasian, he wrote to her on June 14, 1839: "...'This is the day the Lord hath made.'.... I have just said Holy Mass. We are off! Once again, adieu! Yours, heart and soul, after Jesus and Mary, — Joseph, S.M."

The voyage was a long, rough one. Father Chevron had plenty of leisure to pour out his heart in beautiful, long letters to his mother. They are brimming over with picturesque descriptions and amusing anecdotes. In one letter he describes mealtime on the rough seas, "when the ship is tossed about like a piece of kindling wood."

"Just make a mental picture," he says, "of a long dinner table pitched at an angle of about 90 degrees. The plates are tied down snugly by two or three strings drawn lengthwise along the table. The cups and glasses are placed in trays hanging from the ceiling. When you go to sit down, there goes your chair against someone's shins, while your neighbor's chair makes a center rush and tackles you below the knees.

"It is considered a real achievement to hold your soup plate in equilibrium for any length of time. I was trying hard to do this when suddenly a whole basketful of cookies spilled its crumby contents all over my cassock and a steaming dish of baked potatoes followed in hot pursuit. Everyone had a great laugh.

"But 'he who laughs last laughs best.' Our good-natured captain was crimson with laughter at this and other incidents caused by the rough sea. Then, lo and behold, the climax came like a thunderclap. The ship's prow suddenly heaved high in the air and, down below, a roast mutton by sympathetic movement jumped from the table almost to the ceiling and landed with a gravy splash right square in the captain's face."

After a voyage of more than four months, the Australasian reached Sydney on October 29 and from there Father Chevron went to join Bishop Pompallier in New Zealand. The Bishop was a secular priest who had preached several missions with the Marist Fathers in France and had directed the first fraternity of the Third Order of Mary in Lyons. He had come to Oceania with the first group of Marists in 1838. Father Colin, from a motive of humility, had preferred that a secular Bishop accompany his first missionaries.

In Sydney, Father Chevron also met Brother Attale, a Marist lay brother from Grenoble, France, who was destined to be his right-hand man for many years. Together the three of them set out for Wallis and Futuna.

Trouble was in the air. Father Peter Bataillon, S.M., the tall, stalwart missionary of Wallis, who was later to succeed Bishop Pompallier as Bishop of Central Oceania, was the center of a storm of pagan hatred that threatened the growing group of Wallisian Christians. It was Satan's supreme effort for Wallis. The ship had no sooner brought Father Chevron and Brother Attale safely to Wallis, than rumors of a night attack on the boat reached them. The pagans wished to capture the supplies of food that were being brought to the Catholic Mission and also the crew's firearms which they intended to use against "the white man's God."

Father Chevron wrote: "Our catechumens seem quite resolute in the face of this great danger. They keep asking us if they will go to Heaven should they be killed in battle. As for us, we feel quite secure under the loving protection of Mary, whose cause we are defending. And this is her beautiful month of October too. God be praised!"

From Wallis, he and Brother Attale went to Futuna where, in the school of Father Chanel, they continued learning the secrets of missionary life. What a joy it was for the priest of Futuna and his companion, Brother Nizier, to have the company of these other Marists for a few months. Memories of home no doubt came back to all of them like visions. But their mutual joy was short-lived. Great things had happened in Wallis and Father Bataillon wrote to Futuna for help.

"The entire population," he reported, "with the exception of King Lavelua and some members of his family, have become Christian. A banner of the Blessed Virgin has been carried in triumph the length of the island by fervent, happy neophytes."

It was a great sacrifice for Father Chanel to send Father Chevron back to Wallis (it is such consolation to have at least one confrere!), but without hesitation he wrote a letter which Father Chevron delivered to Father Bataillon:

"Dear Reverend Father, We are deeply interested in the marvelous work you are doing, so I am willing that Father Chevron and Brother Attale should leave us to share your labors and your consolations. The news of the conversion of your island seems to have stirred the hearts of our Futunians, but alas, our poor King appears to feel honor bound to follow the example of Lavelua..... Some of the natives have threatened to roast the young men who joined the catechumens who came to us from Wallis. This has intimidated them a little. God grant that the example of your catechumens will give them strength. Father Chevron will have both good and bad tidings of our island, but I am confident that the fervor of your neophytes will in the end work the conversion of Futuna."

Blessed, self-effacing martyr! Nothing but the shedding of his own blood was, in the end, to work the conversion of Futuna! His island, stubborn and hostile until the last, was purchased by his death just a few months after he bid his confrere goodbye.

Father Chevron wrote to his Superior General, Father Colin, in France: "It was with deep regret that I left Futuna, where Father Chanel was being cruelly persecuted. One thought consoled me — that I had sacrificed the crown of martyrdom by my obedience, the greatest sacrifice a missionary could make. Four months after my departure my saintly brother received the palm refused to me."

Not long afterward he responded as generously when another sacrifice was asked of him. He was happy in Wallis but his Bishop now summoned him for the important expedition to Tonga. He wrote to his mother: "I'll never be able to tell you how hard it was for me to leave Wallis. Father Bataillon came aboard to say goodbye. I tried to speak, but I couldn't. There were too many lumps in my throat..... Braver than I, he said to me, 'Cheer up, dear confrere. Yet another sacrifice, and the last diamond will be set in your apostolic crown!'.... I asked God to give me more mastery over my poor heart.....and then, suddenly, like the sun bursting through the dark clouds, the beautiful words of Our Lord flashed through my mind: 'And everyone that hath left house, or brethren, or sisters, or father or mother.....for My name's sake shall receive a hundredfold and shall possess life everlasting.'"

Tonga was indeed the last diamond in his apostolic crown. He spent 42 years working there, without ever returning home to France, and his body still rests in the picturesque cemetery in the great Catholic town of Lapaha. A simple, wooden cross is planted in the white sand of his grave.

CHAPTER 5

NAPOLEON OF THE SOUTH PACIFIC

THE FIRST TONGAN CATHOLIC was Fieota'Anga (meaning one who loves to eat raw sharks), the young wife of Moeaki, chief of the town of Pea. She was baptized about a year after Father Chevron's arrival and given the Christian name of Aloisia (Louise). All of her children and twenty-nine other relatives were also baptized at the same time. A few months later her husband and forty of his men followed her good example.

Years later, Louise Fieota'Anga enjoyed telling the younger Marist Fathers how Father Chevron spent his first night in her husband's house. He and Bishop Pompallier and their party, after that first Mass on the morning of Our Lady's Visitation in 1842, made an official visit to Nukualofa. They approached the capital with apprehension, remembering a most uncordial reception that the Bishop had been given five years earlier when he called on King George Tupou I in Vavau, requesting permission to establish a Catholic mission there.

King George the First, from whom the pressent Tongan royal family is descended, was born in 1787 and died in 1893 after a life as eventful as it was ever given a man to live. George Tupou the Second, who died in 1918, was his great-grandson and the father of Her Majesty, Queen Salote.

Taufa'Ahau, as he was known before he became a Christian, was King of Haapai in the barbarous days when Haapai, Vavau and Tongatapu were three distinct kingdoms. His childhood had been spent among scenes of famine, bloodshed and horrors introduced from Fiji, where boys of his age were taught to torture wounded prisoners. When other boys were playing with toy canoes, he was joining his father in night attacks that made his name a terror to the other islands. He grew up into a powerful young warrior with a lust for conquest, surpassing his fellows both in stature and in all sports that demanded skill. He was only 23 years old when his father died.

The young ruler of Haapai, awaiting an opportunity to further his ambition — the conquest of all Tonga — in 1826 heard of the arrival in Tonga of representatives of the Methodist Society of England. Did he have an intuition that this new religion, supported by a powerful nation, was a means to attain what his heart yearned for? He sent for one of the missionaries, was instructed and (says Sir Basil Thomson in his book, "Diversions of a Prime Minister") "as soon as he understood the new religion's teachings he signed the death warrant of the old. . . . In a land where might was right . . . . . the whole island of Haapai was soon entirely Protestant."

Five years later King George visited Vavau and persuaded the king of that little nation to come over to the new religion. When the latter died not long afterward, George became ruler of the two kingdoms, Haapai and Vavau.

Tongatapu (Tonga, the Sacred), however, still remained largely pagan. Its king, Aleamotu, was Protestant, it is true, but many of his chiefs, seeing in the new religion, championed by the powerful King George, a force that would eventually destroy what little sway they still had over their people, remained firmly aloof from the new movement. Gradually the pagan opposition centered in the well fortified towns of Pea and Houma. But after several years of warfare, accompanied by horrible cruelties, the terrible king of Haapai and Vavau finally managed to subdue his enemies and take up permanent headquarters in Nukualofa.

He was exultant with victory, but his joy was by no means perfect. Deep in his heart was a bitter feeling of wounded pride, occasioned by the obstinate resistance of the town of Pea. With its deep trenches, its palisades of coconut tree trunks stoutly bound together, its huge walls of coral stone, often as much as fifteen feet thick, its outposts armed with sharp pickets of iron wood, Pea was, in its native way, a truly formidable fortress.

This last stronghold of paganism was called "the Devil's Camp." It was destined, in the plan of Divine Providence, to become the cradle of the Catholic Church in Tonga.

Happily, King George was absent when Bishop Pompallier and Father Chevron and their party visited Nukualofa on July 2, 1842. Aleamotu, still nominally king of Tongatapu, received the Catholic missionaries quite graciously. Bishop Pompallier presented a huge kava root to him and officially requested his permission to establish a Catholic Mission on his island.

"Nukualofa has already received the Englishman's religion," they were told. "But Pea is still pagan. You had better go there." Two messengers were sent to the Devil's Camp at once. The people of the renowned, fortified town received the news with lively enthusiasm and welcomed "the great white chiefs." And none was happier than Fieota' Anga, wife of Moeaki, the chief, who had dreamed that someone would come to heal all of her children with a sacred water.

Chief Moeaki's reed-built hut was given to Father Chevron for his dwelling, the gift signifying that the Catholic Mission, which the priest represented, would be protected by this brave warrior's people. His Lordship, Bishop Pompallier, celebrated Mass publicly, as the crowning event of the jubilant reception festivities, and the people were greatly impressed. Then the overjoyed prelate bid farewell to Father Chevron and Brother Attale, and returned to his headquarters in New Zealand, thanking God that the hour of salvation had come for the Tongan Islands.

According to custom, Fieota'Anga gave her guests mats to sleep on that night. No sooner had Father Chevron settled down to rest than he became aware that his bed was inhabited by certain little unfindable creatures. So, when he thought everyone in the house was asleep, he arose quietly and went outside to recite his Rosary.

Fieota'Anga told the Marist Fathers years later how she peeped cautiously through the reed wall of her own hut and stood there observing the young priest in silent admiration. It was a beautiful, calm night. As the golden globe of the full moon's quivering light shone through the trees, softly reflecting its silvery sheen on the white stranger's uplifted face, it seemed to her that she saw not a man but an angel. She awoke her husband, who also admired him and felt strangely moved as he wondered how those slowly moving beads could cause such sweet peace and happiness to be reflected in the priest's face.

While they were watching, a messenger arrived from Nukualofa with a counterorder, commanding Moeaki not to receive the strangers. King George had returned!

The next morning a great "fono" (gathering of chiefs and people) took place. Father Chevron was invited. The chiefs seemed to hesitate between their fear of King George's wrath and their desire to keep the missionary in their midst.

Father Chevron arose and told them: "This hesitation that I see in you proves the love you already have for me. I am greatly touched, and I'm resolved, for my part, never to leave Pea. Only sheer violence can tear me away from you. If necessary, I'll willingly give my life for your eternal happiness and that of all the Tongan people."

His words went straight to the heart of Moeaki, who arose and with ceremony thanked the priest. "No one hesitates any longer," he declared. "You will stay with us. You will teach us your religion. You will bless us. And if we are attacked we shall die together!"

The news spread through the island like wildfire. The usual calumnies against the Catholic Church had already filtered into the islands, but they were in vain. The mustard seed of Faith was planted in Tongan soil. The great work had begun. The Church had come to stay.

Only God will ever know the hunger and thirst, the ridicule and mockery, the suffering and sacrifice, the love and zeal, the optimism and cheerfulness in spite of all, that filled those first hard years of apostolate for Father Chevron and Brother Attale. Father Jerome Grange, S.M., was their first helper. Other Marist Fathers, bound for other islands, who visited the little mission, wrote: "What a joy it was to see our dear confreres again! And yet, what a sorrowful meeting it was! They were so thin and worn out with fatigue and privation that we couldn't help weeping for sympathy."

Another visitor wrote: "No matter how destitute the poor you see in France may be, their poverty is nothing compared with that of our Tongan missionaries. More touching still is the way they try to keep their hardships and privations secret, for fear they might be sent to another and better mission!"

The Tongans called Father Chevron "Patele Sevelo," the nearest their language could come to the French name, Chevron. He worked so continually and so untiringly that they wondered, "How can Patele Sevelo live without sleep?" Kava parties, public meetings, private interviews, sick calls — all these were for his burning soul so many golden opportunities to preach "Jesus Christ and Him crucified." Night and day he was always ready to receive any Nicodemus and talk religion in that quiet, simple way the Tongans admired. Day by day, little by little, almost imperceptibly, God's grace penetrated their hearts, through the saintliness and constant zeal of His missionary.

A beautiful Tongan-style church was built at Pea where the little flock continued to increase. Using the old fortified town as a center, the missionaries went to all parts of the island. In 1845, three more churches were built, one at Hologa, near the great sacred village of Lapaha; one in Hahake (Eastern Tonga), in the village of Kotogo; and one in Houma, on the western coast.

When a fanatic set fire to the Hologa church and burnt it to the ground, Father Chevron left that village and went to live in Lapaha, home of the Tui Tonga, the great "spiritual king," whom the natives believed to have an immortal origin. The first long-ago Tui Tonga, they believed, "dropped from the sky one day," according to Father Peter Castagnier, S.M., who died in Vavau in 1910.

The Tui Tonga took a fancy to Father Chevron the first time he saw him. He liked his simple ways, his kind loving face, the earnest look in his eyes. Time after time the missionary tried to teach him the great truths of our religion but he would only shake his head. No, he would remain faithful to the religion of his forefathers. He considered this new religion as an influence and power bound to destroy his despotism. Father Chevron only prayed harder. And finally the last of the sacred Tui Tongas became a child of the Church through Baptism.

Father Chevron wrote to his family in France: "....One day I resolved to make one last supreme effort. Confiding myself to our Divine Mother's protection, I went to see him (the Tui Tonga). There I did my utmost to win him over to our cause, showing him the advantages of the Catholic Faith, not only for his own personal salvation, but for the temporal and eternal welfare of his people.

"Alas! all my reasoning left him cold and unmoved. I was about to go when suddenly a look of compassion gleamed in his eyes. It was a sign of his love for me in spite of all. Then I made a fresh appeal, entreating him, if ever he had any love for me, to stop the agony that his indifference, hesitation and cold silence were causing me to suffer.

"Oh, the wonderful power of God's grace! The Tui Tonga arose, grasped my hand and promised that before the week was over he would put his name on the list of those preparing for Baptism. The next Sunday he made his solemn entrance into the Catholic Church by coming to Mass with twenty members of his household." (Quoted from Father Monfat's "Les Tonga.")

The news spread like lightning all over Tonga. The Catholic chiefs of Pea came in joyous haste to congratulate him in the Tongan way — by bringing immense quantities of cooked food and large, well cooked pigs.

Meanwhile, the clouds of prejudice and religious bigotry that had been gathering finally broke into the storm of another war. King George distributed muskets and advanced on Pea. Our Fathers were summoned to leave the fort. They replied, "Catholic priests do not abandon their flock in the hour of danger! We shall stay at our post until death!"

The clever, warrior-king, by a ruse, persuaded the chiefs of Pea to attend a parley in Nukualofa. They went in all confidence but, in their absence, the wily king's warriors stormed the old fortress and soon the cradle of Catholicism in Tonga was a mass of flames.

King George himself happened to meet Louise Fieota' Anga as she was fleeing from the burning inferno. He stopped her and tore the Rosary she was wearing from around her neck, threw it on the ground, stamped upon it with fierce hate, and shouted, "Enough! From now on, no more Rosaries! No more Catholic Church in Tonga!"

Many Catholics were banished to Haapai and Vavau where their Acadian-like exile proved a providential means of spreading the Church, in spite of all opposition. Those Catholics who remained in Tongatapu were forbidden to wear scapulars, medals, etc. The persecutors thought the mission could never recover from such a blow. But the wild storm of persecution served, as persecution always does, only to further the designs of God and strengthen His Church.

Catholicism was banned everywhere throughout the kingdom except in Lapaha village where the Tui Tonga lived. Here Father Chevron and his assistants took refuge. Here they continued working, praying, preaching, remembering that Father Colin, their Superior General and founder of the Society of Mary, had always said that persecution and apparent defeat were sure signs of ultimate victory for any new foundation, just as the ignominy of Calvary preceded the triumph of Easter.

Father Chevron composed a Tongan grammar and dictionary. In the classical language of Lapaha, he wrote many hymns and sermons explaining the principal truths of the Catholic Church. His hymns are the pride of present-day Tongans. About two hundred of his sermons also survive, all neatly written and excellent in form and subject matter.

One of his assistants was Father A. Lemaze,

S.M., who later became the first Bishop of Central Oceania. Bishop Lemaze wrote: "I consider it one of the greatest privileges of my early missionary life to have spent fifteen happy years as Father Joseph Chevron's assistant. He was a splendid missionary, a fine companion and a wonderful scholar in the beautiful Tongan language. He was also an admirable Marist, who really lived according to the spirit of our Society, the spirit of humility, abnegation, intimate union with God and ardent love for souls. In spite of grave difficulties, he always managed to be faithful to the daily religious exercises prescribed by the rule of the Society. He loved Our Lord in the most Blessed Sacrament so much that he spent at least two hours each day in the church."

And that, of course, is the secret of Father Chevron's success as a missionary — his active ministry was but the overflow of his deep and genuine interior life.

As a final proof of his devotion to his adopted people, he asked to be buried according to the Tongan custom, with no casket but wrapped instead in tapa cloth and mats. Amelia, the Catholic Queen of Wallis, provided the mats and tapa cloth that were used for his burial. Among his pall bearers were Tungi, a Protestant chief, and Gu Tupou Malohi, a grandson of King George.

In his old age, King George learned to love

the Marist Fathers and the Sisters of the Catholic Mission, and to appreciate their good work. He enjoyed having them come to his palace and talk about Napoleon. The old warrior would chuckle with delight and, recalling his own many wars and conquests, jokingly call himself "the Napoleon of the South Pacific."

He became particularly attached to one missionary, Father Armand Olier, S.M., who later became the second Bishop of Central Oceania. Patele Olie, as everyone called him, would come to the royal palace and spend hours there laughing and chatting with the old king. One day Patele brought his royal friend a present, a beautifully bound volume, well illustrated with many pictures, the "Lives of the Saints" written by Father Thomas in the Tongan language. Whom do you think King George picked out as his favorite saint? The gentle little poor man of Assisi, St. Francis!

Sometimes the king returned Father Olier's visits by strolling down to the Catholic Mission in Maufanga, not far from Nukualofa. He was greatly interested when they built the new church there. A coral-stone building had never before been erected in Tonga. One day he went up to one section of the rising walls and tried in vain to shake it with his strong shoulder. When he found it immovable, he smiled his wonder and admiration at Brother Charles who was in charge of the work.

The laybrother and his novice-masons were, of course, much pleased at this encouragement from the king.

The old man was also interested in the Maufanga Brass Band which Father Olier organized and trained. His son, Prince Uga, was a member of the band. He thoroughly enjoyed the story they told him of the band's first trip through the islands. The natives, of course, had never seen "ukamea piko" (crooked pieces of iron) that could make music. When they called unexpectedly at Haapai, and anchored in Lifuka harbor, the musicians started to play a solemn tune from the ship's deck before going ashore.

The natives thought Judgment Day had come and that this terrific rumpus was Gabriel's horn. Pandemonium followed. Shrieking with terror, some climbed to the tops of the highest coconut trees. Others ran in frantic tumult to the deepest part of the jungle.

Father Olier promptly stopped the music, went ashore with Prince Uga, and explained to the chief that it wasn't the end of the world at all, but only a brass band. The "lali" (wooden bells) broadcast the message and the people returned, so happy to be alive that they immediately prepared a huge festival with plenty to eat, as is the custom.

King George, in his old age, did much walking and thinking. He was still tall and straight, with a surprising vigor and sprightliness. He was accustomed to take a daily plunge into the sea. As he walked in the cool shade of the stately row of tall Norfolk pines, along the palace road, no doubt he not only reviewed his own eventful past but also thought much of his soul's future, for he was intellectually as energetic as he had been in other ways.

He knew, from both his Protestant teachers and his Catholic friends, that when his long life ended, as it must do soon, he would meet his Maker face to face. A great change had taken place in his mind and heart, since Father Chevron's time. He could see now that the Catholic Missionaries whom he had persecuted were, like the saints whose lives they had given him to read, followers of Christ who loved sinners so much that He visited in their homes and shared their meals.

As a result of his deep friendship and close association with Father Olier, King George had come to the point where he definitely expressed his desire to become a Catholic and promised Father Olier that he would do so. He never actually took that important step but all missionaries who have lived and worked in Tonga, and grown to love that little kingdom and its people, hope and pray that the day may not be far off when some of his descendants will, by the grace of God, embrace the Church the old king learned to love too late.

CHAPTER 6

THE DOCTOR DANCED A JIG

ANNA BOYER was a beautiful, 18-year-old half-caste girl; when they told me she was dying I dashed off down the coral stone highway on my new bicycle in answer to my first sick call in Tongatapu.

It was early morning in Nukualofa, the beautiful little capital of a beautiful little kingdom. The coolness of night still lingered, as if loath to leave, and air-conditioned the calm, sweet scented dawn. The sun's first bright rays were breaking through the branches of the shade trees — banyans, mangos, breadfruit trees — and gently kissing their dew-drenched foliage, as well as the grass, the flowers and the plants of our Catholic Mission compound. The young missionary, enjoying all this for the first time, felt instinctively that this was the beginning of a perfect day.

Just listen to the magic music of the song birds. Did you ever hear anything so gay? Look at the diamond-like sparkle of that cool verdure. All nature seems to be saying its morning prayers, smiling as only nature can smile and softly whispering ever so reverently, "Good morning, God! Good morning, Creator of Heaven and earth! Isn't it good for all of us to be here?"

What is that "tap, tap" sound coming from all over the village? Oh, that is tapa..... But wait a minute..... The young priest opens a little book called "Mariner's Tonga" and reads that 19th-century British lad's description of just such a Tongan morning: "Early in the morning, when the air is calm and still, the beating of tapa (a native fabric similar to cotton, but not woven, being rather the texture of paper) at all the houses about has a very pleasing effect. Some sounds are near at hand; others are almost lost in the distance. Some are a little more acute; others more grave. All, with remarkable regularity, produce a musical variety that is agreeable, accompanied as it often is, by the singing of birds and the cheerful, luxuriant tropical scenery."

Suddenly my reading reverie is interrupted by the arrival of a panting boy who hands me a note that reads: "Father, please come quickly. Anna is dying in the hospital."

What a shock for a young missionary! I had met Anna only the day before. They told me she received Holy Communion every morning. She

seemed as healthy as she was pretty. And now.....
she was dying! How could it be? How could anyone be dying on such a wonderful morning when everything seemed teeming with life and joy?

A rush to church for the Holy Oils and the Blessed Sacrament. A fervent whispered prayer of thanks for the brand new bicycle. A swift ride to the trim Nukualofa hospital on the edge of town. Within a few minutes I was in a neat little room where a strong smell of chloroform filled the air.

A devout Tongan mother knelt in silent adoration as she realized the priest was carrying the King of Kings. There, in a nice white bed, was Anna. My, what a change! What a difference from yesterday! A greenish pallor was on her face; ice-cold beads of perspiration on her forehead. In her big brown eyes was the glassy stare of a person near death. But, thank God, she was still conscious. She made a heroic effort to receive the Last Sacraments as reverently as possible. Her childlike resignation was beautiful — her deep faith and loving confidence in God's holy will.

The natives of Oceania may not be as "civilized" as we of the West would wish them to be. They may still be primitive, very primitive, in their ways and methods of living. They certainly lack the modern comforts and gadgets that we, in America, pride ourselves on. But they are wiser, in the truest sense of the word, than many millions of us for, through the grace of God and the faithful use of this grace, they have learned and remembered that the real purpose of man's existence is to know God, to love Him, to serve Him here below and to be happy with Him forever in the next world. What else really matters?

Unfortunately, however, many of them are still afraid of European and American medicine and methods of medical care. They've had their own remedies for centuries. Frequently there is a battle for a patient between the Tongan medicine man and the doctor trained in modern methods. The doctor sometimes appeals to the missionary to side with him. But if the medicine man wins the argument and the patient dies, he shrugs it off with: "You should have called me in sooner."

The doctor had left Anna's bedside just before the priest arrived. He had scolded Mele (Mary), Anna's mother. Hadn't her daughter already had two attacks of appendicitis? Hadn't he begged her and her husband to let him operate? They had refused. Like so many other good natives, they knew nothing of appendicitis and thought their own primitive remedies were better for their daughter's ailment. Their ignorance was not culpable as it would have been in people familiar with modern, scientific, medical care.

They had refused and now, many hours after this third attack, they were dragging Anna into the hospital in this terrible condition. An emergency operation had revealed a burst appendix and general peritonitis. It was too late. No hope whatever to save her. Her fever was almost 106. "Oh, why, why did you wait so long?" Doctor Minty moaned as he walked out of the room, a look of despair on his face.

After the nurse had whispered this explanation of affairs to me, I went back to Anna and her mother. Mele must have read my thoughts. She knew that I felt her daughter was beyond all human hope, so she called me over to where she was standing and said, with a big, joyous smile that I shall never forget, "Excuse me, Father. Anna will not die. Look, Father."

She held up her rosary beads, indicating that she was storming Heaven, that the Blessed Mother would understand and grant another mother's prayer, that little Anna would not die. The Mother spoke with such deep conviction and such vibrant faith that I felt something tingling inside me like an electric shock. Right here before my eyes was that same faith so often spoken of by Christ, the faith of all the sick who came to Him, the faith of the poor blind man by the roadside, the faith of the centurion, the faith of the lepers, the faith of that dauntless woman who whispered in her heart, "If only I can touch but the hem of His garment....." Surely God would reward such faith as this. He had done it many times. He would do it again.

The Doctor Danced a Jig!

I put a little relic of St. Therese of the Child Jesus under Anna's pillow and promised the mother and daughter that tomorrow morning the Holy Sacrifice of the Mass would be offered for their intentions.

At seven o'clock next morning the nurse came in for her routine check-up. She took Anna's temperature. "Impossible," she murmured. She shook the thermometer and took it again. For the second time it registered normal!

"Anna, how do you feel?" she asked. "Your temperature is normal."

"I feel fine," the girl replied, "but I'm hungry."

The astonished nurse telephoned to the doctor. He didn't believe a word of it. He had to come over to see for himself.

"Doctor, I took it twice and it's normal! And she says she's hungry!" the nurse exclaimed.

Doctor Minty shook his head and went to his patient. One look at her — one good check-up with his own thermometer — the evidence was indisputable! He was so utterly happy that, like a little school boy receiving permission to go to the baseball game or the circus, the dignified Chief Medical Officer of the Kingdom of Tonga promptly danced a jig around Anna's bed.

"Anna, my girl," he shouted, "something wonderful has happened to you! You had a high fever and now your temperature is normal. Your peritonitis condition has vanished completely. I can't understand it! I can't understand it!"

All the while, Anna's mother, her precious rosary still in her hand, was quietly weeping with joy and gratitude to God. After the doctor left and she was alone with her child she said, "Anna, God heard our prayers. How good He is to us! Did you notice what time it was when the nurse came to take your temperature? It was just about the time Father's Mass was ending."

When the doctor discharged Anna from the hospital about two weeks later he told her, "Go straight from here to your church, Anna, and thank God for your miraculous recovery. He cured you. I didn't."

That was more than thirty years ago. Anna and her mother are still thanking God. Both were alive and vigorous when I came home from Tonga in 1951.

CHAPTER 7

THE BOY WHO NEVER GAVE UP

AFTER ABOUT TWO and a half years in Tongatapu I made my first cruise through the entire Kingdom, visiting our Missions in Haapai, Vavau, Niua Foou and Niua Toputapu. It was to have been a one-month trip, but it turned out to be more than three months before we got back.

Would you imagine it could take us eighteen days to cover the ninety-odd miles from Tongatapu to Haapai? Our Haapai Mission knew the day of our departure and you may be sure they were anxious, waiting for us in vain for more than two weeks.

The evening of the same day we left Tonga we sighted Haapai and they sighted us. But it's impossible to go through the narrow pass at night that leads into the anchorage. So the Captain of the "Melrose," a good-hearted, six-foot American, judged it prudent not to go in too close, and gave orders to "lay off" during the night.

After a while it started to rain and an extraordinary current set in. The first thing we knew we were surrounded by menacing reefs. The only thing to do was to set about and beat back toward Tonga, and return at daybreak.

The next day the wind was blowing the wrong way for Haapai, so on we went with this same wind, hoping it would soon shift to a favorable angle. But it was the same all next day and for almost two weeks we went on and on, seeing nothing but sky and sea.

On the fifteenth day we ran into a storm, or a storm ran into us — I couldn't say which — and we were tossed about in amazing shape. The sea on all sides was like a huge, greenish mass of ever-moving mountains. It was almost impossible to eat and we had to nail boards along the side of our bunks for fear of being thrown out of bed during the night.

On Trinity Sunday the wind was so strong that a huge gaff broke in two and fell on deck, nearly hitting one of the crew. Now gaffs on four-masted American schooners are no small pieces of timber. This particular one was of Oregon fir, 35 feet long and almost a foot in thickness.

On the next day the wind changed around at last. How happy we were! Three days later we were in sight of Haapai again, and this time we sailed into port safe and sound. The government authorities were just ready to send a message to Nukualofa, asking that a warship from Fiji be sent out to look for us. No one here remembers such an adventure as we had — eighteen days between two ports, a distance that ordinarily can be spanned in a day.

But come up on deck with me and admire the scenery as we sail into the port of Lifuka. Yes, that beautiful island lying before us is the main island of the Haapai group. From a distance these tropical islands look like so many huge baskets of beautiful greenery with flowers emerging, as if by enchantment, from the variously tinted waters.

Do you see those red-roofed, white-walled houses? They are the homes of the local traders. Farther up on our right, close to the white, sandy beach, is a beautiful, Gothic-style, concrete church. On one side of the church, within the Mission Compound, is a humble dwelling, the Father's house. On the other side is a new and spacious building, the Sisters' convent and school. There were no more than 150 Catholics on the little island then, so this neatly established mission was rather remarkable.

Its pastor was Father Jean Baptiste Mace, a zealous French Marist, who had been miraculously cured of tuberculosis at Lourdes during his seminary days. He had been in Tonga about fifteen years, most of the time alone, without a confrere. How glad he was to see one now. His pale, emaciated, white-bearded face was all smiles. He was about 50 years old, but looked like 75. We embraced a la francaise and off we went to the Mission, amid the smiles and hearty greetings of the natives.

Father Mace told me he had just come from his plantation in the bush, where he was obliged to work several days a week to make ends meet, both for himself and the convent. Only God knows all that those exiled Fathers endure in those tiny, far-scattered islands, where their very separation from confreres is in itself a source of untold sacrifice and merit.

Our first visit, when we arrived on the Mission Compound, was to the hidden God in the Tabernacle, where we knelt for a few minutes in thanksgiving for our safe arrival. If those high Gothic vaults, arches and huge pillars of the church of Haapai could have spoken, they would have told of the heroic labors of that handful of Catholics who built them under the direction of courageous Father Augustin Kervegan, S.M. (God rest his soul!)

Next we went to the convent of the Marist Missionary Sisters, where Father Mace introduced me to Sister Romuald, the Superior, whom Father Mace called his "policeman"; Sister St. Yves, foundress of the Haapai convent, who was then more than 80 years old; and Sister Josephine, an intelligent Tongan nun. We met some of their girls too, who were well trained and remarkably disciplined. Such schools are the backbone of our Missions. Father Mace remarked, "Here in the Missions, the Catholic schools are the doors to the Catholic Church."

Soon we saw people coming into the yard with kava roots to "tali" (receive) the new "Patele Amelika" (American Father). They were a lively looking group, these Haapai Catholics. They had suffered more for their religion than people in other places.

I spent several days with Father Mace in Haapai and we enjoyed many happy hours together, many kava parties and visits around the island. Father Mace told me of his boyhood in France, how he had to be sent home from the seminary because he had tuberculosis. He tried a second and a third time, but each time his health failed. His right lung was gone and the other was finally attacked by the terrible disease. But did he get discouraged? Did he give up? Not Jean Baptiste Mace! For in his heart, like a bright star shining, was a firm trust in Our Lady.

He went to Lourdes and, kneeling before the beautiful statue in the grotto, he poured out his soul to Mary Immaculate. "Mary, Mother dear, please cure me! Otherwise how can I ever become a priest and go to Oceania to save souls for whom Christ died?"

He went back to the seminary with his left lung cured!

Eventually he was ordained and became a Marist missionary. Obedience and Divine Providence sent him to the Tongan Islands. He was fired with a burning desire to spread the Faith and his heart was filled with deepest gratitude to Our Lady of Lourdes, Queen of the Islands of the South Seas, where he was to spend the remaining years of his life.

For thirty-one years he worked there in his humble, quiet, cheerful way, always kind and fatherly. Two years after my visit to him in 1924, he was sent to remote Keppels Island, his last field of labor, and I became his successor in Haapai. For almost twelve years he lived in Keppels, founding the convent of the Marist Missionary Sisters there, rebuilding churches and establishing schools, even starting a new station on a beautiful mountain called Tafahi.

Once, for almost two years, Father Mace never saw a fellow priest. Yet he loved confreres so much! He enjoyed cracking jokes with them and singing comical old French songs. His nearest neighbors, during those years at Keppels, were Tin Can Island, 107 sea miles away, and Vavau, 166 miles to the south.

One village in particular will never forget Father Mace — the village of Hihifo, Keppels. That's where he founded the convent and built the cutest little white coral-lime church you could ever imagine. Can you guess to whom he dedicated that church? Yes, Our Lady of Lourdes! While the work was in progress Father Mace was sometimes terribly ill with fever but he wouldn't give up. He insisted on being carried to work. When the building was finished he put a fine, bronze statue of Our Lady of Lourdes on top of it — a statue that looked over the whole island and far out to sea toward all the islands of Mary's living Rosary of Oceania.

Once, when he was ill with fever, a sick call came. He had the natives lift him up into a dump cart, the only kind of transportation in Keppels. They went very slowly, fearful of hurting their Father. When he arrived at the patient's hut he had just enough strength to hear the Confession. Then he fainted, and when they brought him home the Mother Superior thought he was dead, he was so pale and lifeless.

But God had other plans for His faithful servant. Father Mace had been so generous with Him all through his life that his Heavenly Father willed a more consoling death for him. He who had been so kind to the Sisters in Keppels was to die surrounded, as it were, by a living wreath — the seven Sisters of the Vavau Convent.

"I feel like a school boy going home for vacation," he said just a few minutes before he died in 1942.

And he left a little school boy behind — a lad he had once brought with him to Tongatapu from Keppels, a little boy who, when he grew up, was himself ordained a priest and who was for a time pastor of his native island of Keppels, Father Petelo Maka Mei Moana (Stone From the Deep).

CHAPTER 8

THE HERMIT OF VAVAU

THE SCHOONER was sailing for Vavau and Father Mace was going to Niua Toputapu, so after a few days in Haapai, off we went together. That very night we covered the ninety miles between the two groups. When morning came we saw Vavau's beautiful port and capital city, Neiafu. The port is so large and so well protected by picturesque mountains that it could easily hold all the navies of the world. The trim little village and the fleet of small sailing crafts lying at anchor near the concrete wharf were a wonderful sight that clear, cool Sunday morning in July, 1924.

The captain took us ashore in his launch so we could say our Masses. At the top of a graceful slope leading up from the mirror-like waters of the harbor, was the Catholic church. And there was Father Kerrman coming to meet us — Father Kerrman, who had reminded me of St. Francis de Sales the day I arrived in Nukualofa almost three years before. He was pastor of Vavau and, like Father Mace, all alone. His thoughtfulness and delicate charity made our visit to Vavau a pleasant one.

The Sisters, at that time, were not so well housed as in Haapai, although now, thirty years later, their convent is a fine two-story building, one of the best in the Kingdom of Tonga. The new convent is the work of Father Francis Deguerry, S.M., who was pastor there at a later date than Father Kerrman. In 1924 the Sisters' house was situated at the bottom of a mountain and when it rained the yard was so muddy that sometimes the Sisters would lose their shoes. Their girls were quite numerous and, as in Haapai, very well trained and disciplined. What a happy influence the holy lives of the nuns have on the characters of their sometimes wild-natured pupils!

One day Father Mace and I went up to the summit of a mountain in our Vavau Mission property to visit the Catholic cemetery. With its neat sand mounds and quaint-shaped crosses, its splendid site overlooking the beautiful, lake-like harbor of Neiafu, the Mission cemetery here was perhaps the prettiest in all of Tonga. We paused before a small, nameless cross and a large, white sand grave carefully covered over with small black pebbles. Reverently taking off his hat, Father Mace said, his voice betraying deep emotion, "This is Father Breton's grave."

Father Joseph Breton, S.M., was the founder of the Mission in Vavau. During the long years he spent there he lived like the hermits of old in the desert. The people at that time (1863 — 1881) were still savage and rude. In vain he tried to spread the Gospel of the true Faith. No one would listen to him. True apostle that he was, he soon realized that it was not through preaching that he could convert them, but by hidden penance and sacrifice.

When, at rare intervals, Fathers from other islands were privileged to visit him, they always found his cooking utensils rusty and his kitchen filled with cobwebs. His Lordship, Bishop Armand Lamaze, S.M., who was Vicar Apostolic of Central Oceania from 1879 until 1906, visited Father Breton in 1880 and he reported: "His ordinary food and drink consisted mainly of hard sailor's biscuit, coconut meat and water, with oranges. He only used his kitchen when he had to make hosts for the altar. Poor Father! He slept very little and his bed was much harder than that of a Trappist. He spent the greater part of the night in prayer before the Blessed Sacrament. What is still more touching is to see the radiant happiness, the whole-hearted joyfulness, we always find in him."

The natives thought Father Breton was demented and called him "vale" (foolish) because they said "he hardly ever ate, never got impatient, and prayed all the time."

Another priest who visited him said, "At Vavau we found the holy Father Breton, a real hermit, an example of Marist humility, of extreme poverty, of love which gives itself utterly, a continual adorer of Jesus in the Blessed Sacrament."

His was an apostolate of suffering, a sanctity won through failure. "I am here alone, where God has put me, through the will of my Bishop," Father Breton said. "I shall stay here willingly until I die. I do very little. I can show no brilliant conversions. But if I suffer with patience for the glory of God and His holy Mother, I hope that my life at Vavau will not be altogether useless for His glory and the salvation of these poor souls."

He was 66 when he died in 1881. He died as he had lived — alone. His nearest confrere was 150 miles away and no one in Tongatapu knew of his death until after he had been buried. Prisoners dug his grave. A Protestant chief performed the burial service. The Premier of Tonga, the Honorable Shirley Baker, also a Protestant, preached the eulogy. He was indeed a true Marist, hidden and unknown to the very end. But God has His own ways of avenging His servants.

As Father Mace and I stood beside Father Breton's humble grave that July day in 1924, he told me this story:

"Father Breton had been dead 27 years and Father Peter Castagnier, S.M., one of his successors in Vavau, was gradually approaching his last moments. I was pastor and young Father Deguerry, newly arrived from France, was my assistant. According to the Tongan custom, we wished to prepare Father Castagnier's tomb beforehand.

"We consulted our Bishop, Monsignor John Olier, S.M., about the matter and he wrote us from Nukualofa to bury Father Castagnier along with Father Breton. We explained to him how small Father Breton's tomb was but the Bishop, for some reason, insisted.

"So Father Deguerry and I came up here, followed by a crowd of natives, both Catholic and Protestant, to see what state the tomb was in. After the white coral sand that covered the tomb had been removed and the huge flagstone turned over, like a sudden vision, half frightening us, the remains of Father Breton's body appeared to us apparently intact.

"But as soon as I bent down to examine them more closely, they crumbled into dust. Only the head remained whole and it had an opening in the forehead. It was a moment of deepest emotion for everyone. At first the natives were struck with awe and remained silent. I felt that I must perform my delicate task quickly. Soon I had gathered all the precious remains and placed them reverently in a small casket that we had prepared for that purpose.

"The natives were by now very excited and their faint whisperings grew into loud murmurs. Father Deguerry and I wondered what it meant. As we nailed the cover down their murmuring grew louder and their gestures more excited. We wondered what was the matter and what they meant, as they kept repeating, 'Loto o Patele.' We were both still quite unfamiliar with their language and we didn't know that one of the several meanings of the word 'loto' in Tongan was 'brain.'

"Finally we understood by their gestures that they had seen something wonderful and wished us to open the casket again so they could show it to us. So we opened it and were greatly astonished when we noticed for the first time what the keen eyes of the natives had spied from the beginning. Through the opening in Father Breton's forehead, the brain could be seen intact! I took it up in my trembling hands. It was still soft and spongy and life-like — not in the least decayed!

"Our emotion reached its climax when, with one accord, the natives cried out, 'This is the answer of Heaven in behalf of him we used to call foolish!'

"Father Deguerry and I were puzzled as to what should be done. Some of the Catholics wanted us to bring the relic to the church. We both felt like doing so but, remembering the wise laws of our Holy Mother the Church regarding such things, we decided to draw up a Latin formula testifying to what we had seen, get some natives, both Catholics and Protestants, to sign it, and seal this document in a glass jar along with the precious remains."

You can imagine how I felt at hearing such a wonderful bit of history related by its principal witness there at the very scene where it had occurred. Then and there was born within me a deep feeling of love and veneration for that unknown, saintly confrere whom it may someday please God to canonize through the voice of His Church.

EIGHTEEN YEARS LATER I saw with my own eyes Father Breton's still intact brain. His tomb was again opened, this time at the request of Father Mace who, just before he died, asked to be buried with the holy hermit of Vavau. "Be sure to look in the glass jar," he told Father Kerrman and me.

It was a bright summer morning in 1942 when we carried out his instruction. The natives were there in large numbers. Father Breton was buried very deep by that time, perhaps nine feet or so. This was because each year, on All Souls Day, as is customary with them, they had cleaned the grave of every growing thing and brought up fresh coral sand from the seashore to spread over it. The accumulation of sand, down through the years, counteracts the natural erosion caused by the rains; the mounds grow higher and higher and the graves become deeper and deeper.

The "haatufunga" (ceremonial undertaker) went down into the grave, took the glass jar out of its little casket and lifted it up so all the people could plainly see it. Father Kerrman and I, of course, were deeply thrilled to see for ourselves the amazingly preserved relic. And this was more than a quarter of a century after Father Mace had held it in his trembling hands — sixty-one years after the priest they called "vale" had died all alone after eighteen years of hidden penances and sacrifice for the glory of God and the salvation of the people of Vavau.

CHAPTER 9

THE SAINT OF TIN CAN ISLAND

TWO HUNDRED MILES northeast of Vavau is the isolated island of Niua Foou, better known as Tin Can Island. Niua Foou means "new kind of coconuts." The island was named for the remarkably fine coconuts grown there.

The name "Tin Can Island" originated because of the island's peculiar mail service. Out-going mail used to be sent off by natives who swam out to a passing steamer with the scanty letters tied on the end of a stick which they tried to keep out of water. Each swimmer in turn dropped his little parcel into a can lowered from the ship's side. Then the in-going mail was thrown overboard in a sealed tin can which the natives pushed before them as they swam back to the treacherous shore about a mile away.

Tin Can Island is also an active volcano. From a distance, its huge, steaming mass, with its shock-rent rocks and rugged coast-wall of black lava cliffs, ever white-fringed with angry breakers, seems to rise out of the mild Pacific like some gloomy and fantastic fortress.

Traces of volcanic action are everywhere. A severe eruption took place in 1853 when a village was destroyed and many lives lost. On April 12, 1867, another eruption occurred but no one was killed. But old Tin Can really blew its top in 1942 when a terrible eruption destroyed all the government buildings and forced the inhabitants to evacuate. They now live on Eua Island, at the southern extremity of Tonga's 150-island kingdom.

After our visit to Vavau, in July, 1924, Father Mace and I sailed for Tin Can Island. We could have landed the next day after we left Vavau if someone had been there to show us where to cast anchor, but it was five days later before we managed to get ashore. There were only two possible spots where a vessel could anchor. One was on the west side, at Futu, where a depth of fifteen fathoms could be found at a distance of about a cable from shore, but that was too close to be safe. Forbidding, black lava rocks lined the shores all around the island. Landing was hazardous at all times and sometimes absolutely impossible.

The other, by far more dangerous still, was at a village called Agaha. We had sailed past Agaha without being able to go ashore, although we were so close that we could see the crowds gathered to watch us. We could even distinguish the cassocks of Father Pierre Jouny, S.M., and his assistant, a native priest from Wallis, Father Petelo Moa Aka Aka (the Hen Who Kicks). We were unable to make a second attempt that day, for darkness set in, along with a bad wind and rain, so we had to lay off for five days on the sheltered side of the island.

On the fifth day, while making another attempt to reach the anchorage, we picked up a small boat with a long, lanky Tongan in charge, who called himself a pilot. Events soon proved that he knew more about planting yams than he did about piloting. As we approached the jagged, jetty-like, black lava rock that marked the unsafe anchorage of Agaha, the pilot, standing alert at the prow, gave orders to cast anchor. Down and down it went, sixty fathoms and yet no bottom. The captain ordered it to be stopped and roared his anger at the fake pilot.

Father Mace and I were beginning to think we might have to wait another five days before setting foot on Tin Can Island when we spied a "popau" (Tongan canoe made from a hollowed tree trunk). We knew the two half-naked natives who manned it were Catholics because they were wearing scapular medals. We hailed them to come alongside, and jumped in the canoe with them. Before the captain or anybody else could dissuade us, we were skimming up and down the huge, dark blue swells and heading straight for shore.

As we drew near the wharf our skillful oarsmen waited for a favorable swell, then swept inland on its crest. Strong and eager hands were there to receive us — Father Mace with the first swell, then myself on the second. It was an exciting moment, as you can imagine. Almost before we realized it we were landed high and dry and standing before the smiling crowd of strong-armed natives who were enjoying our expression of mingled surprise, fright and thankfulness.

As we gazed upward to the top of the high plateau, wondering how we could ever climb up there, Father Petelo came down to greet us and led us triumphantly to the smiling crowd above. Five minutes later we were on the Mission Compound.

There on our right was the wooden church building. It had been completely overturned by a hurricane in 1918 (six years before our visit), but was now completely rebuilt and looked quite new with its fresh coat of white paint. A few paces ahead of us, near some storm-tortured ironwood trees, was a little old gabled house with a rusty tin roof and decayed veranda. It was Father Jouny's dwelling. On our left was a Tongan, leaf-covered structure, Father Petelo's rectory.

Father Jouny was pacing up and down the veranda, so attentive to the recitation of his breviary that he had not seen us coming. He was almost 80 years old, the oldest Father in the Tongan group, and he had been on this wild, volcanic island for more than 38 years. When he spied us, his venerable countenance, with its long, patriarchal beard, beamed into one big whole-hearted smile. He ran forward to embrace us, tears of joy gleaming in his paternal eyes and trickling down his worn cheeks.

How can I ever tell you the deep impression this meeting with Father Jouny made upon my soul? As we saw him there before us, in his greenish-black, oft-mended cassock, and barefooted, we instinctively felt that here before us was a living saint, a model missionary, a twentieth-century St. Paul. We understood immediately the beautiful meaning of the quaint expression our Bishop often used in reference to him: "Father Jouny is the lightning rod of our vicariate. The merits of his holy life draw down upon us the blessings of Almighty God and shield us from the just punishments of His holy wrath."

How good it was to converse with this venerable confrere, to ask his advice, to see how truly happy he was in spite of his poverty and privations. How inspiring to meet a priest who had personally known our Father Founder, the Venerable Jean Claude Colin, and the other Fathers who had formed the new little Society of Mary almost a hundred years before — our predecessors whom we had only read about in books.

Simple, kind, completely forgetful of self, ever filled with joyful and confident optimism — that was Father Jouny, founder of the Catholic Missions of Niua Foou and Niua Topatapu.

He was born in Plougenast, a small town in Brittany, in 1846, just five years after Blessed Chanel's martyrdom, the seventh child of a simple Breton family. He made his profession in the Society of Mary in 1872, taught theology for two years in France, and then sailed for the Oceanian mission field. For ten years he was the Queen's chaplain on Wallis Island, that "paradise of consolations" for all missionaries who go there.

Then he was called upon for another and more complete "giving up of all for Christ's sake," and sent to the isolated islands of the Tongan Kingdom. When he first went to Keppels, no one wanted to give him a place to build his hut, so he made himself a reed-built palace on the sands of the seashore. He used to tell, with a twinkle in his eye, how one day he saw his hut swept away by the sea when the high spring tides came.

At Tin Can Island his reception was even less enthusiastic. Food was still more difficult to obtain than it had been in Keppels. But he toiled day in and day out, in the terrible heat of that tropical sun, to grow his own yams, sweet potatoes, taros and other food. He was of a frail build and unaccustomed to manual labor, and his hands blistered and bled.

No doubt he often wiped the perspiration from his brow, paused a little to rest, his eyes scanning the distant horizon where the dark blue of the ocean mingled its tints with the azure sky, while his thoughts traveled on beyond hundreds of other hidden horizons until they rested on a little workshop in Nazareth where Someone Else had toiled for His living and Someone Else's Hands had blistered and bled too. That vision kept Father Jouny smiling, for he knew he was following the Master. All through his fifty-seven years of missionary life in one of the most difficult posts of the Pacific, he kept smiling and making melody in his heart, conscious that he was following Him all the way and winning souls He had died to save.

One day someone was congratulating Father Jouny on the numerous conversions he had made. Tears filled his eyes as he answered, "Only recently it has been so — only since the Little Flower began her mission in Heaven. She is the one to congratulate."

Good Father Jouny! Living prayer, living psalm, living model of the self-sacrificing missionary! How truly and fondly the Little Flower must have loved him — another "Little Flower" sprung from her own French soil and transplanted to Oceania when Little Therese was only one year old — another soul with a child-like simplicity and burning love of God just like hers.

In the last few years before Father Mace and I visited him in 1924, Father Jouny had begun to reap what he had sown, both in Tin Can Island and Keppels. Almost half the latter island was then ready for conversion, as we learned when we went there soon after.

"Come and see our church," the dear old priest joyfully invited us that July day. I'll never forget what we saw — four bare, paintless walls of rough pine and a poor altar of worm-eaten wood painted over with old gray paint. On the Gospel side a piece of rough crating was nailed to the edge of the altar shelf. On this was an old, oily, smoking storm lantern — the sanctuary lamp! As we went out, after a moment's adoration in this poor, Bethlehem-like abode of Jesus, Father Jouny optimistically inquired what we thought of his church. We dared not tell him, and hastily changed the subject by proposing a visit to the Sisters.

Again what poverty we saw! And yet what cheerful neatness! The veranda was so decayed that we had to watch our step lest we should go through. When we entered the parlor — a tiny room about eight feet by twelve — Sister St. John blushingly apologized as she offered us her only substitute for chairs — kerosene cases. These we joyfully accepted as "just as good."

Sister St. John's only companion was a 50-year-old Tongan nun, Sister Makalita (Margaret) who, incidentally, died on June 30, 1952, while this book was being written. We told her all the news about her relatives and her home in Tongatapu.

Sister St. John, who was born in Australia, of good old Irish stock, inquired about Nukualofa where she had once been superior of the Girls' School, and also about Ireland. When I noticed her extreme poverty and suggested that she write home to Australia about her mission, she replied with deep and sincere humility, "It is better to suffer in silence and remain unknown."

Four miles from Agaha, the capital, was the village of Futu. As we approached that village with its quaint, brown-leaved Tongan huts, the little tots came out to greet us, crying gleefully, "Ko Patele! Ko Patele." (It's Father! It's Father!) Then the grown-ups came to receive us with kava roots in their hands and keenest delight on their faces.

Soon we were seated in the shade, near their large stone church, enjoying a good "Fai kava" (kava party). The catechists and others made speeches and then someone got up to make a "kole" (beg a favor). This is a real art in which the Tongans excel.

Theirs was a good and reasonable "kole." The orator explained how their church was incomplete. Its chief builder and architect, a good Wallisian, had been called home by God before he finished his task. There was the bell, weighing half a ton, to be lifted up to its position in the bell tower. The four-masted schooner on which we had come to Tin Can Island had brought two beautiful stained glass windows for the sanctuary.

Now who in all Futu knew anything about installing bells and stained glass windows? There was an oratorical pause. Then the "kole" to "Patele Etuate" (Father Edward), begging him to do this work for them. Of course I was only too happy to accept, so it was decided that I should stay in Futu until the work was finished.

I had almost the entire population of the village at my command those four days I spent in Futu. Women from various sections of the town brought me six meals a day. Each time I had to taste everyone's cooking lest the good matrons be offended. Fish, fowl, pork, white fat worms, yams, bananas, sweet potatoes, eggs from a bird called "malau" which lays its eggs in the ground and leaves them there to hatch — such was the general run of the daily menu, **a la tongienne.**

They prepared a wonderful bed for me in the little Tongan house I occupied during my stay. In the corner were piled dozens and dozens of red-fringed mats, carefully laid one upon another, and covered with large pieces of well-decorated tapa and a good, soft pillow. Wasn't that a bed fit for a king?

Every evening after supper and night prayer, the people would gather around in a grand old kava party until bedtime about 10 o'clock. We talked of many things. They asked me questions about my home in America and about the Catholic Church. They were delightful evenings, filled with sweet, home-like joys. A missionary learns many important things on such occasions that he could never learn otherwise. When the work was finished and I went back to Agaha, Father Jouny was again brimming over with happiness.

The captain of our ship, the Melrose, came to see us and was greatly impressed by what he saw. He told me, "Father, I've seen a good many missions and I've met a good many missionaries in different islands of the Pacific, but I've never seen a poorer mission than this one. This Father Jouny — why, he's a saint, that's all! Never have I met a missionary who deserves help as he does."

He handed me $25 saying, "Here is a small offering in the name of the ship's company." When Father Jouny received it and heard of the captain's kind words, tears gleamed in his eyes and, forgetting himself in his joy and gratitude, he disclosed a secret we would otherwise never have learned. "How good God is!" he exclaimed. "I haven't had a penny in the house for more than three months! God will bless this good captain for his charity!"

Three days later we left him. When I was sent to Haapai two years afterward, and Father Mace was assigned to Keppels, Father Jouny, leaving Tin Can Island in charge of his successor, Father Kerrman, went to live on Keppels too, so Father Mace would have "a confrere to go to confession to," as the old priest put it.

On Christmas Eve, 1930, as Father Mace and his growing flock were preparing for Midnight Mass, a violent hurricane broke loose on the island. Father Mace wrote to us afterward: "We had to move Father Jouny three times in the middle of the night, through the worst part of the storm. He might have been killed by the falling debris of our house which was totally wrecked. Finally we carried him to the church where the Catholic people had taken refuge.

"There, while the terrific storm was tearing off clanging sheets of iron roofing and scattering them like leaves through the devastated island, Father Jouny, cold to the very marrow and exhausted with fatigue, slept like a child just a few steps from the altar.

"I hardly dare speak of the following months. I suffered so much because I could not give our beloved confrere the care which his great age and fast-failing strength demanded. How could I? All we had to give him was fish and coconuts.

"He gradually became so weak that I thought it prudent to administer Extreme Unction. His last agony lasted four days. Nobody here ever saw a dying man so low, yet so resistant against the clutch of death. He couldn't pronounce a word or even swallow a few drops of water, but he was fully conscious. Whenever I said my breviary he would ask, by a sign, for his own and hold it in his trembling hands.

"On the fourth night of his agony, while the natives and I were reciting the 'Memorare', that beautiful little prayer to the Blessed Virgin, Father Jouny breathed his last like a little child going to sleep in his Mother's arms. It was July 12, 1931."

Should you ever go to Keppels to visit his grave you'll find a little white mound of coral sand with a simple wooden cross marking the place where Father Jouny sleeps. His life remains an example and inspiration for the confreres he left to reap where he had sown. Charity obliges us to keep praying for the repose of his soul, yet we hope that he, whom both Catholics and non-Catholics called "the Saint of the South Pacific," has already received his eternal reward.

Just a few months before he went home to God he promised, "When I die I will do like the Little Flower..... if it is God's holy will..... I will spend my heaven praying for Oceania."

THERE HAD BEEN no resident priest and no Sisters in Keppels for ten years before our visit there in the summer of 1924. Yet we found the best Catholics of the whole Tongan group on that remote island. Why? I believe it was because the two founders of the Catholic Church there, Father Jouny and Father Joseph Berger, S.M., had such great devotion to the Sacred Heart. Our Lord promised, you remember, through the little Visitation nun of Paray le Monial, to those priests who had devotion to His Sacred Heart, special graces for touching the hardest of human hearts.

In the few years (1905-1914) that Father Berger spent in Keppels, he accomplished an amazing amount of good, both materially and spiritually. He had complete control over his Catholic people and great influence with the entire island. The fire of zeal burned brightly in his apostolic heart. Those Tongan hearts, ordinarily quick to forget, still cherished his memory and remembered his words of deep wisdom and experience.

They said he had the gift of prophecy. They said, at whatever time of the night they came to him for medicine, he was always dressed and ready to help. They said that, after his death which he had clearly forseen and prepared for, they found a sharp, iron-pointed belt around his waist almost buried in his flesh — testimonial to the power of penance. They said that one Holy Thursday after he died the candles on the altar lit up by themselves during services presided over by a catechist, and strains of heavenly music were heard.

They told many things about Father Berger. I wish I could have met him. But for Father Mace and me, the greatest proof of his saintliness was that which we saw with our own eyes, when we found how full of faith and fervor his shepherdless flock still remained after he had been dead ten years.

We preached a most consoling retreat there every evening for an entire week. The church was crowded with both Catholics and Protestants. We found the Protestants well disposed and seemingly almost ready for conversion. Father Mace and I resolved to do our utmost to persuade our Bishop, in spite of the scarcity of priests and nuns, to send a Father and Sisters to that distant island as soon as possible. We felt that if our request should be granted, the island was practically ours — or rather, the Sacred Heart's!

Early in September I left Father Mace in his Haapai home and boarded a cutter for Tonga. As we neared Nukualofa harbor, we saw there was great excitement on the wharf. We soon learned the cause. An 8000-ton steamer that we had noticed the night before, lying motionless on the distant horizon, was a wreck. With hundreds of passengers aboard, at midnight it had struck the dreaded "hakau fisi" (the reef we had fled from three months before), but thanks to a warship in Nukualofa harbor its wireless distress signals had been heard and all lives saved.

A few hours later I reached Maufanga feeling like a cross between the prodigal son and a weary tramp, glad to be home again after so many adventures. And how my little flock rejoiced when I returned to the village of Houma, where I had a little Tongan house of my own. The people rushed out on the road to greet me, as if I had been gone for years. Eagerly they grasped my hand and cried joyfully, "Malo aupito hoo folau lelei mai! Fakafetai kihe Eiki!" (Congratulations on your happy return! Thank God for His protection!)

How happy we all were, the Father and his children! They came in great numbers to Confession and Communion. The Sacred Heart had watched over them well during their Father's absence, but now he was home ready to work harder than ever to spread His reign in Hihifo, the smallest and poorest district in Tongatapu — ready to preach and hear Confessions, to offer the Holy Sacrifice every morning and give the Bread of Angels to the brown-skinned children of Hihifo, to administer the last rites to the dying and to baptize dear little brown babes whose large, bright, black eyes were full of Heaven.

Coming home is always the best part of every voyage!

CHAPTER 10

ONE FRESH EGG FOR THE BISHOP

EVERYTHING WENT WRONG the first time His Excellency, Right Reverend Bishop Joseph Blanc, S.M., head of the Vicariate of Tonga, came to visit my newly founded mission station at Houma, in the southwestern part of Tongatapu. It was my first foundation and therefore my first love.

(Admonition to all future missionaries: Everything you learn — Greek, Hebrew, Epistomology, Liturgy, everything — will be useful to you in the mission field. But there's much more besides, that you'll have to learn the hard way — in the school of experience. You'll see what I mean. . . . .)

I was as busy as the proverbial bee, building this and that, making cement tanks for our fresh water supply, putting up schools and dormitories, shifting buildings from several miles away. (Folks had said they couldn't be shifted.) I was feeling pretty perky and proud of myself. You begin to think you're quite a guy, you know, and then God in His great goodness sees that He's got to prick this little bubble of your secret pride. So He whispers to the Bishop, "How about going over to Houma and visiting that young man from the United States? Go see for yourself how things are shaping up in his new station."

The Bishop thought it was such a good idea that he wrote a note to me and sent it by a boy on horseback: "Come with your Ford car and bring me over to your Mass next Sunday. I will preach the sermon and after Mass we'll have breakfast together."

"Delighted," said I to myself.

Then a shade of worry crept into the picture. We had no Bishop's throne. There wasn't even room for an episcopal canopy. There were many other things we didn't have. This was a new bush parish. The church itself was just a Tongan hut, enlarged all around by a sort of lean-to barely seven feet high. We did have a nice big statue of Our Lady of Lourdes. Behind it was a hen's nest. The hen had decided this was about the safest place in the world to lay her eggs.

Well, about seven o'clock Sunday morning I cranked the old Model T Ford into sputtering life and went down to Nukualofa, eight miles away, to fetch my ecclesiastical superior. I explained to him about the absence of the throne and he assured me an ordinary chair would do. I didn't dare tell him about the hen that might be coming in about Mass time to lay her daily egg. I just kept hoping that she mightn't come at all when she saw a strange man dressed in purple so near her nest.

We had no sacristy, so I had to vest behind the altar. When the altar boys were ready, out we went to the sanctuary where the Bishop was awaiting us. We forgot to bow to him, of course. In my best Sunday voice I intoned the Asperges and then....and then.... According to the rubrics, the priest must never, never sprinkle the Bishop with holy water. Instead, he hands the Bishop the aspergillum and the Bishop sprinkles himself. But did I remember that? No, I proceeded solemnly to sprinkle the Bishop.

A look of startled surprise came across his face as the first drops struck him (or so it seemed to me), and he motioned for me to stop and give him the "stick." A little voice inside me chided, "Why didn't you look up the rubrics when you knew he was coming?"

The painful silence that followed this incident (noticed of course by the keen eyes of my native parishioners) was suddenly shattered by the vigorous and triumphant cackling of that blessed hen! She was just a foot or so behind the Bishop's improvised throne. Bishop or no Bishop, she decided at that moment to broadcast to the whole world that a wonderful thing had happened — she had laid a nice big egg!

From then on things went quite normally for a while. The Bishop preached such a fine sermon and made such a deep impression on his listeners, that I completely forgot the first bad break I had made and promptly plunged into a still worse blunder by turning around at the end of Mass and giving the last blessing to the people, hen, Bishop and all — something else that the rubrics forbid. The Bishop should have blessed everyone instead.

I thought I heard a little gasp as the gravity of this mistake dawned on me. (It could have been my imagination of course.) All during the Last Gospel I seemed to feel the Bishop's eyes drilling two little round holes through the middle of my back. It was most embarrassing — to put it mildly! Here was the first chance my Bishop had ever had to bless my flock. And here was I, through sheer forgetfulness of elementary ecclesiastical and liturgical politeness, robbing him of his right and depriving my people of an episcopal blessing. Horrible thought!

But more was yet to come. It seemed to be one of those days when things start going wrong and keep right on going from bad to worse. While I was making my thanksgiving after Mass, the Bishop was waiting for me under a tree. I thought he had joined the party of natives who were ready to start making kava, as they always do on Sundays. At last it dawned on me that I was not only keeping him waiting but hadn't even thought how hungry he must be after that 8-mile ride over those rough roads in the brisk morning air.

So I hurried out and apologized, "My Lord, please excuse me. And excuse the Sisters for being slower than usual this morning. No doubt they're preparing something special in your honor. You'll have at least one fresh egg!" He smiled at that, and I felt a little better.

Soon a little tinkling sound told us that all was ready. So we went in for breakfast — nice hot coffee, fried eggs, toast..... But something was lacking.

"There's no milk, my Lord. I'm sorry. You gave us a cow last month, but this morning, of all mornings, I forgot to milk. I'm very sorry, my Lord."

After breakfast the Bishop went upstairs to his room and I went to mine, as we both had our breviary to read. It had been arranged that I would take him home after lunch. About 11:30 I thought he'd be free, and wishing to make one good impression on him, I decided to ask a favor in a very, very liturgically correct way. I had intended asking permission to erect the Stations of the Cross in our new bush chapel. So I got a book and faithfully copied out a beautiful Latin formula which began: "Ad pedes amplitudinis tuae provolutus (prostrate at the feet of your greatness), I beg permission..."

I handed him the note, thinking it would please him immensely. He read only the first line. Then quietly and tersely but with a faint twinkle of amusement, he informed me that I had copied the wrong formula. "This one is used only for the Pope. You'd better go back and write another note in a language you understand better than Latin."

This was the last straw for the camel's back of my pride. The bubble burst at last. The big balloon of egoism exploded.

After the Bishop blessed our frugal lunch, I suddenly gave the table a good sharp punch and said in a loud voice, "My Lord, I am disgusted! I'm very angry... at myself! Everything has gone wrong that could possibly go wrong! I sprinkled your Lordship with holy water. The hen laid an egg during Mass and boisterously told everybody about it. I robbed your Excellency of the first chance to bless my people. I forgot to milk the cow. I copied out a Papal formula instead of the right one. Can anything happen that hasn't already happened today?"

Then the Bishop burst out laughing and, with a few words, put me at ease. We had a fine time together from then on. When I had delivered him safely back to Nukualofa, I told him, "My Lord, do you know what I'm going to do tomorrow morning? I'm going to offer up the Holy Sacrifice of the Mass for your intentions — and mine — asking God to give me more common sense, to help me learn the rubrics a little better, and to prepare for your next visit a little more thoughtfully."

He smiled an indulgent smile and replied, "Thanks, Father! That's an excellent idea! Goodbye now and God be with you!"

CHAPTER 11

A LEPER WHITE AS SNOW

HOLY MASS IS OVER in our little village chapel in Folaha, Tongatapu. Will you go with me to visit a leper? Don't be shocked. Leprosy isn't nearly as contagious as it has been considered for centuries to be. But the undeserved stigma of the disease still clings, in civilized and uncivilized nations alike.

There's really nothing new under the sun. Remember, in the days of Our Lord, when He was going about doing good, how the poor lepers were unwelcomed outcasts? And how He loved them so much? Well, in tiny Tonga when someone is found to have leprosy his family hides him deep in the woods, hoping against hope that no one will hear of it. For they are ashamed and mortally frightened, ignoring the fact that leprosy is not at all so dangerously contagious as tuberculosis which they hardly notice until it reaches the last stages.

Poor lepers! How glad they always were to see a Catholic missionary, who wasn't afraid to come near them, shake hands with them — yes, or even kiss them. I did that once, just to show up the leper's family who were watching from a safe distance, and to make them realize how silly their fright was. The little act of kindness had farther reaching results than I dreamed, for it proved to be the beginning of the leper's conversion. He died a most edifying death, not long afterward, in that earthly heaven for lepers, Makongai, Fiji.

I was always glad to hear someone whisper to me of the whereabouts of a leper and, no matter what religion he was, I made a point of visiting him and giving him little gifts.

This time we're going to visit Tupou who is a Catholic, about 35 years old. Are you ready to go with me? We're taking the Gift of Gifts, Our Blessed Lord Himself. Two red-cassocked altar boys lead the procession of the Blessed Sacrament Which the priest is carrying on his bosom. See how the catechist and a few braver Catholics also follow, as on and on we walk through the tall woods and shaded, vine-clad forest.

On and on we go with Jesus, just as of old when He went to see the lepers. The tiny bell the altar boy is ringing awes the song birds into silence and seems to say at each of its tinklings, "Jesus is coming! Jesus is passing by! The King of Heaven and earth is going to kiss a leper!"

Yes, he may be living alone in the deep woods. He may be an outcast whom everybody shuns with fear. But Jesus knows where he lives. And today Jesus is going to make a tabernacle, a living ciborium, out of this poor leper's mangled body.

Now we are near his little grass hut. See there, through that coconut grove. As he hears the silvery tinkling of the bell, his soul and his poor body quiver with deepest joy. From his heart springs the cry of the blind man of the Gospel, "Jesus, Son of David, have mercy on me!"

Yesterday, when I came to hear his Confession, he was startled when he saw the old model T swing in alongside his hut. It made so much noise and its radiator was steaming like a tea kettle. But it could turn on a dime and go easily through bushes and tall grass. He cried out, telling me not to come in because he was fearful of contaminating me. But of course I went right in and shook hands with him and sat down beside him and heard his Confession. He was weeping with sheer joy when I left, promising to bring him Our Lord this morning.

Now, as the priest enters the little hut, the leper's face is again streaming with tears of joy. How reverently he receives Holy Communion! With what rapture he makes his thanksgiving! The group of Catholics who have been brave enough to come near him wait outside and sing appropriate hymns.

Yes, he may be just a poor leper, just an outcast, but the terrible disease that wrecked his body has strangely purified and beautified his soul. In the tabernacle-like stillness and solitude of his jungle home, in the lone hours of sleepless nights, he has learned the great secret of life — death to self by wholehearted love of God.

He has with him the "Kau Sagato" (Lives of the Saints), the Gospels in Tongan, the "Tohi Kole," (a fine Tongan prayer book), and his Rosary. But what has contributed most to his sanctification is his isolation and solitude, the treasures that monks and hermits have voluntarily sought through all the centuries of Christianity.

He has heard the saying, "A friend in need is a friend indeed." He has learned that God has not abandoned him, even though his people have; that He is indeed his only true Friend. Today, more than ever before in his life, Tupou, the leper, realizes that Jesus, his changeless Friend, who comes to him both sacramentally and in the person of His "other self," the priest, is his only "Friend in need."

Father Tabb wrote these immortal lines about another leper, Father Damien:

"Oh, God, the cleanest offering
Of tainted earth below,
Unblushing to Thy feet we bring,
A leper white as snow."

Now aren't you glad you came with me to visit Tupou?

It doesn't seem that it happened as long ago as 1925, in Tongatapu, just before I was sent to Haapai. It was the first and last time I gave him Holy Communion, for I left shortly afterward, and he was sent to Makongai, in Fiji. I saw him there, in the leper settlement, in 1951. He is an old man now — a good old man who has learned what many people never learn, that suffering, lovingly accepted, tends to make us see clearly and thereby brings us closer to God, while sometimes joy and too much prosperity have the opposite effect.

CHAPTER 12

THE HORSE DIDN'T GENUFLECT

IF YOU EVER GO to Tonga you won't be able to find, in all that little kingdom, any other people who give so much time and attention to Our Lord in the Holy Sacrament of the Altar as those of Lifuka, Haapai, where I was pastor from 1926 until 1951. Father Herman Joseph Therriault, S.M., of Lille, Maine, is now serving the people of Lifuka.

In no other place will you find the Association of the Knights and Handmaids of the Blessed Sacrament established. In Lifuka, the Corpus Christi processions are the most elaborate and the repository on Holy Thursday the most gorgeous; the singing is the most beautiful and the Holy Communions the most numerous in proportion to the Catholic population.

All this is largely because the horse didn't genuflect, "Marist Topix" notwithstanding. That bright and sparkling little magazine, published by students at Marist Seminary in Washington, D. C., somehow got hold of the story of the horse and printed it in their July-August 1952 issue. But they were misinformed, and when I read that article, entitled "The Horse Genuflects," I nearly jumped out of my chair.

In all my talks about Haapai I had never once spoken of this story. It was taboo (or tapu, as the Tongans would say). But I had to put "Marist Topix" straight. The old nag didn't genuflect. I know, because Kelemete Vahai, the present catechist at Lifuka, who was only a boy at the time of the historic incident, told me the whole story.

But now I'm glad "Marist Topix" brought it to light because otherwise perhaps you would never have heard of this wonderful instance of the mysterious ways of Divine Providence, which can make use of a missionary's mistake, an old nag and a genuine, but perhaps not very guilty, apostate for the good of souls and the ultimate glory of God.

The church in Lifuka, dedicated to Saint Teresa of Avila, a fine bit of mission-style Gothic architecture, is there today and filled to capacity with Catholics who are devoted to Our Lord in the Blessed Sacrament, just because that horse did not genuflect.

Its owner tied the nag to a post for three days. Why did he tie him to a post? To make him fast.

(Excuse the pun.) I mean he wished the animal to abstain from food. Why did he want to make him fast? Well, it was because of an argument between an unbeliever and an impulsive and excitable missionary, Father Augustine Kervegan, S.M., from Bretony. (R.I.P.) It happened back in 1911, the year of Haley's Comet, the year of my entrance in Marist Seminary, and other important events (ahem!).

Poor Patele Aukusitino! You see, he was alone, 100 miles from his Bishop. (A good distance to be in some cases, for both parties concerned, but there are exceptions, and this was one of them.) He had no confrere to advise him. And he loved Our Blessed Lord so much that he simply lost his head. In vain the Sisters tried respectfully to point out the folly of his wager. The catechist also pleaded in vain. Father Augustine stuck to his plan in spite of all the prayers and pleadings of those who knew better.

To prove the Real Presence of Our Lord in the Blessed Sacrament, he had rashly arranged to carry the Sacred Host in procession down the road past the place where the horse was tied. On one side of the road would be a big bunch of bananas hanging from the bough of a tree; on the other, the hungry nag. When the priest approached, the horse was to be untied and Father had promised, "Before going over to eat those bananas the horse will first genuflect before the Blessed Sacrament." (Gee wiz! But let's forebear to judge! We are sinners all!)

Of course the news spread like wildfire. Great crowds gathered. Haapai was then a hotbed of the most rabid anti-Catholic feeling. Thanks be to God, it is no longer so! And those two stubborn creatures are in great part responsible for the change — the horse with no human sense and the human with no horse sense. (May the good Lord forgive me — my fellow missionary was holier than I'll ever be!)

Vahai, the catechist, told me, "Instead of weakening our Faith in the Blessed Sacrament, it made it stronger. Do you know what happened? Just as Father Kervegan was about to take Our Blessed Lord from the tabernacle, the sky above the church became pitch dark. A sudden whirlwind started to blow. Peels of terrific thunder were heard. It got so dark that the hens and chickens went to roost in their accustomed places in the trees. I said to Father, 'Patele, God seems to wish to stop us from going out. But he declared, 'No, no, it is the Devil. He's the one who is trying to stop me. And he just won't, that's all!'

"So out we went. I was very frightened. I didn't like to go with Father because somehow I knew it was wrong. The crowd suddenly stopped talking. There was a deep and painful silence. As we approached the horse, someone untied him. He looked at us, paused a bit and then, turning toward the bunch of ripe bananas, walked over and started to devour them.

"War whoops of triumph and blood-curdling yells of sarcasm and mockery filled the air. All the Catholics present were the victims of insults and jeering remarks. They were fighting mad too, and surely there would have been serious trouble if it hadn't been for an important chief who was present, Sioeli, a descendant of the famous Tui Tonga whom Father Chevron had converted. Sioeli was at that time (in 1911) an apostate from the Catholic Church, although some years before he had risked his life in saving the Blessed Sacrament from the blazing church of St. Michael in Mua, Tongatapu. By God's mysterious plan, he was to save Our Lord again."

Vahai continued his story: "If it hadn't been for Sioeli, I don't know what would have happened to us. He came and stood by us with a big club in his hand. With a voice like thunder and eyes glowing with indignation, he cried out, 'Listen to me! What happened just now proves nothing! It proves nothing against the doctrine of the Real Presence! Can't you see that Patele Aukusitino is the one who made a mistake — not the Catholic Church? He had no right to do this! He realizes it now! Every one of you go straight home before I brain somebody with this club!'

"The frightened mob had not expected such an outburst. They began to disperse in sullen silence. Poor Father Kervegan was bent low in weeping adoration. How true the apostate's words were! How they burned and seared his soul! He made his sorrowful way back to his church, almost blinded by hot tears of deepest contrition and crushing anguish of heart. He put Our Lord back into the tabernacle and rang the church bell to call the Catholics.

"When they were assembled he knelt down, facing his people, his hands meeting on the altar rail, and begged their pardon for his rashness. He had tempted God. And God had given him a lesson and admonished him through the mouth of an apostate.

"Everybody was sobbing. They heard the touching prayer of reparation that the poor priest poured out from his aching heart as he turned in the sanctuary and knelt facing the tabernacle home of his pitying Friend."

Was it then and there that he made a vow to erect the beautiful stone church as an act of reparation? I don't know. I do know, however, that shortly afterward Father Kervegan and his little flock started to build the beautiful church of St. Teresa of Avila.

"He would always be the first to work," the catechist continued. "He would insist on doing the hardest jobs, carrying huge boulders and sacks of wet sand on his back. He was a great seaman and captained his own small sailboat. He would sail to an island eighteen miles distant to fetch the huge flagstones for the foundation masonry. Unbelievers marveled at the plan and size of the new structure. Mockingly, they wondered, 'Why do these Catholics, who are only a handful in number, insist on building such a big church? It will never be filled.'

"But the Catholics plugged away and worked with a will together. How could they do otherwise when they had such an example in their pastor who toiled like a Trojan and never spared himself? During the construction period they consumed, not only numberless pigs and goats and sharks and what not, but also FOURTEEN HORSES!"

So if you ever go to Haapai, be sure and visit the little boy from Maine who is now pastor of St. Teresa's Church and get him to introduce you to Vahai, the catechist, and go with them both into the beautiful building and say a little prayer for poor Father Kervegan. Yes, and for Sioeli too.

CHAPTER 13

BETHLEHEM COMES TO TONGA

IT'S 7:30 P.M., MID-DECEMBER, 1951. The missionary, just returned from the South Seas, is wandering and wondering in downtown Boston.

Neon lights, millions of them, all tints and shades and colors, are blinking and flashing. Breathtaking displays and decorations in the big department store windows! Milling crowds, all in a hurry. Endless streams of cars creeping through traffic. And that tingling tang of new-found cold where Jack Frost, just for fun, becomes the big make-up man, rouging everybody's cheeks with a natural, healthy glow.

There's a Christmasy feeling in the air. And white, sparkling snow! Snow, manna-like from Heaven! Snow — Eucharistic whiteness — Nature's swaddling clothes — Mother Winter's masterpiece — an altar cloth crystal-woven for the King of Kings.

"Father," asks a good-natured Irishman (Boston is full of them, thank God!), "Father, how does it feel to be back home again after thirty years in Tonga? What is Christmas like down there in the South Seas?"

A smile of sweet memories lights up the veteran missionary's tanned face. He is back again in his island home. Back again to his first Christmas in Lifuka, Haapai. Twenty-five years ago, but it seems only yesterday.

At first it didn't feel like Christmas at all. It was so hot and noisy. There were the firecrackers and the big bamboo cannons, four inches thick and about five feet long. For a while I was sure someone had made a mistake and thought it was the Fourth of July. Then it dawned on me that I was in the Land of Upside Down. You see, "down under," everything is in reverse. Winter is from June to September, summer from November to April. The south wind is cold as it blows **up** from the South Pole, and the north wind is hot and damp as it blows **down** from the Equator.

"But, Father, isn't it hard? Not having that Christmasy feeling, I mean?"

Sure it's hard, but it's all in the game, as we say. It is part of one's readjustment, one of the first things every new missionary must experience. And it's fun just the same for, after all, what better fun can you have than doing something hard for God?

Christmas Eve, 1926 — what a hectic day! There was the crib to be made. Out it comes from your own workshop, custom-built and ready on the dot for the Sisters, God bless them all. Out come the sheep and the shepherds, the ox, the ass and the camel. What a hit **he** makes with the bright-eyed, brown-bellied kiddies! Then come the Blessed Mother and St. Joseph and finally the Divine Infant. It's worth every minute of the work just to see the delight and awe in the children's big black eyes as they watch Him being put reverently to bed in the manger.

The Catholic Mission Compound is a buzzing beehive of coming and going. The convent girls are sweeping, washing, mending, ironing. Others are sewing at top speed on hand-driven sewing machines, making dresses. They're very good at it too. The Sisters, blue aprons flying, are intent on their respective tasks. One is in the kitchen with the cooks, baking cakes and puddings and making candy and cookies for that big snack after midnight Mass.

Sister Mary Annette, after carefully preparing the twenty-six figures for the new crib, wipes her perspiring face with the corner of her apron and smiles a greeting as she becomes aware of Patele's presence. Then she has a whole string of "kole" (things you ask for):

"Please, Father, do get your boys to prepare us a whole week's supply of firewood."

"And Father, could you make the crib frame a little larger than last year's? And could you rig up a nice little electric light, a blue one, for the inside of the crib?"

"And Father, the 'maile' (evergreens) on Oua Leva Island! It will be low tide at about ten this morning and the boys could cross over on horseback. Tell them to bring us a lot, for we want to make garlands and wreaths for the whole length of the church and the sanctuary."

"Father, please remind the women to come early with their best mats to dress up the church columns."

"And Father, I'm preparing the big ciborium for tonight. I'll send over your clean linen. Sorry, Father, we couldn't mend your shirt so we used it for rags to wash and wipe the windows."

"Sister! That was the only shirt I had left!"

"Yes, Father, but why are you always giving them away? We won't have time now to make you another for Christmas."

"O.K., Sister. It's too hot for shirts anyway."

"By the way, Father, do you hear those bamboo cannons booming? I wonder where they get their kerosene. Every bang is a squirt and every squirt means a whole mouthful. You'd better watch your tin in the refectory."

"You mean, Sister, that I'd better have a squint at where their squirts 'kerosenated' from originally?"

We laugh together.

"By the way, Father, have you noticed how the girls are all keyed up and working like mad? Do you know why? We've got some firecrackers and skyrockets to celebrate with after Midnight Mass. 'Bye, Father. There goes the dispensary bell."

And she's off at top gear. God bless our Sisters. What wonderful workers for God and for souls!

As we cross over to the workshop, a big cart comes into the yard. Two smiling natives are sitting on top of a load of freshly dug yams. This is the beautiful Tongan custom of "polo-polo maala," offering of the first fruits of the land to Patele.

"Thanks very much and God bless you! Your plantation has done very well."

"And here is a basketful of live chickens to go with them, Father, and also some pineapples." Note how Divine Providence works it! This is part of the hundredfold He promised!

The coconut trees are swaying gently in the breeze. The temperature is about $90°$ in the shade. The whole town of Lifuka, capital of the Haapai Archipelago, is teeming with activity. The natives from other islands have sailed in to do their Christmas and New Year's shopping, very careful of their strings of empty bottles, precious things in this part of the world. They will be filled with kerosene for their lamps. After they've weighed their copra and have been paid in money, they will buy knives and spades and axes, tins of corned beef and "ma pakupaku" (hard biscuits), loaves and loaves of fresh bread, toys and fireworks for the children, calico for loincloths and dresses, tobacco and kava — and CHEWING GUM! They haven't got the bubble kind yet. This kind only smacks, but how they love it!

Another boatload of Catholic natives has just pulled in from one of the distant islands. Hungry and wet with salt spray though they be, they are all smiles as they kiss the Patele's hand and begin their litany of "koles."

"Father, there are no more 'kapa pulu' (tins of beef) in the store. Can you spare us some?"

"And some calico, Patele, for my wife and children?"

"Father, may we have some water from your tank?"

"Father, we need some brass polish for the band instruments."

"Father, someone is waiting in church with a baby to be baptized."

"Father, may we borrow your rowboat to go out fishing?"

"Father, Sister wants some small nails and some tacks, six packages of candles and a bottle of altar wine. And she says there are a lot of people in church waiting for Confession."

The church is beautifully decorated by now, fine mats adorning the columns, the crib ready for the "glad tidings of great joy." But first, Confessions and yet more Confessions.

Three hours later there is a clanging sound from the old crankshaft hanging in the refectory. The building is really more like a chicken coop than anything else. That's the "kai" bell. "Come to supper," it says. After a much needed shower and some dry clothes — as a matter of fact, they haven't been dry all day — in we go for a good substantial supper to tide us over. There won't be another meal until about 8:30 tomorrow morning — two sung Masses, one low Mass, three sermons and hundreds of Holy Communions later.

Boom! Boom! The cannons are still at it. The kids are having a wonderful time. They use their mouths as filling cans, to squirt kerosene through a small hole in the base of the cannon. The charge is lit with a match. Who invented them? No one knows. Sometimes I think it was the Devil himself, for they cause many petty thefts of precious kerosene and can be a great nuisance, especially when the gunners go into action without warning and the booming shatters the siesta-time silence, just as one is getting down to forty winks.

"It's getting late now. Ah, there it is — the "lali" (wooden bell) which is sounded at 10:30 p.m. It is soon followed by the big bass drum, calling the band boys together. They look tops in their clean white shirts and white "valas" (loincloths), and do they smell sweet! It's the scented coconut oil in their hair and on their arms and legs. After church they will put a big hibiscus flower in each ear and play tunes around the village until daylight.

At 11 o'clock the church bell rings again and the people enter, singing "Adeste Fideles." It's sung in the beautiful Tongan language but the music is the same familiar melody. Two girls from the convent bring Patele an eggnog and some light food. He'll need it too, for he has a big task ahead of him. He is the only priest within a hundred miles. He has to preach two sermons, one in English and the other in Tongan. He'll celebrate one High Mass and a second Mass of thanksgiving tonight, and then at 7 o'clock in the morning another High Mass and another sermon.

As he vests, with ten altar bays milling around him, the soft strains of the "Adeste Fideles" drift into the sacristy. Then follows "Silent Night," also in Tongan, of course, and sung as never before in all his life he has heard it sung. The whole parish is singing — men, women and children. It sounds like a huge organ made of human voices.

And then something clicks within the missionary's soul. Loneliness falls from him as the thrill of boyhood Christmases steals into his heart again, making him forget the heat and the Fourth of July-like firecrackers, and bringing back the Christmasy feeling. The very air seems filled with singing angels and light and gladness. As the wonderful singing of these simple natives takes him back in spirit to Bethlehem, the hectic day is suddenly forgotten. He hears again the song of the angels and sees the shepherds bent low in adoration. He sees St. Joseph, Our Blessed Mother and the little Jesus Himself, Infant, Savior, God.

"Introibo ad Altare Dei." I will go unto the altar of God.....

A boundless joy and gratitude mixed with wonderment well up in his heart as he begins midnight Mass. He is Mary's own missionary in her coral-island world, her Rosary of atolls strung across the Pacific. Tonight he would not change places with anyone in the whole world.

"Gloria in excelsis Deo....." Glory to God in the highest and on earth peace to men of good will.

The church is packed to capacity with a happy, carefree throng dressed in their Sunday best. A look of serene peace is on every face. They have come to love, to adore, to sing — to sing with all their hearts of glory to God and peace to men of good will.

And there is another reason why they are so happy tonight. Jesus, the One of Whom the angels sang on that first Christmas night — Jesus, the gentle Father and changeless Friend of all, is coming tonight to the manger of their hearts, through Holy Communion. Of such as these humble folk the angels sang "peace to men of good will."

They are only poor natives, just recently converted to Christianity, yet they well know that Christmas means Christ's Mass. They will never know the meaning of the expression "white Christmas." They may never see neon lights or brilliant shop window displays. But they do know, by the grace of God, that the most important thing on Christmas night is to go to Holy Mass and to make room for Him in the inn of their hearts by a good Holy Communion. For this is what Patele has taught them and from the pulpit tells them now:

"E Kainga (Dear Brethren):

"We are here tonight, not only because we are following a sacred tradition handed down to us by centuries of Catholic Faith, but because we know, through the gift of Faith, that the same Christ Who was born nearly two thousand years ago tonight, in a poor little stable, in a hillside cave near Bethlehem, and Whose Divinity was hidden under the appearance of a new-born Babe, is here present on the altar, hidden under the swaddling clothes of the Blessed Eucharist.

"In fact, by a divinely prophetic coincidence, the very word 'Bethlehem' means 'house of bread.' On that first Christmas night the shepherds, eagerly obeying the angels' words, cried out, 'Let us go to Bethlehem.....' We don't have to go to Bethlehem. We are already there. For this is Bethlehem, the house of the Living Bread. This is Jesus, the very same of Whom the angels spoke, 'Behold I bring you glad tidings of great joy....for there is born to you a Savior Who is Christ the Lord.'

"Tonight, are we not doing something more meritorious even than what the shepherds did? After all, they saw a wonderful miracle. They heard the angels singing. The crystal-clear notes of their song seemed to be cascading down from the high heavens like a limpid rainbow of sapphires and diamonds. They saw with their own eyes the most beautiful Baby that ever was born, resting in the arms of the most beautiful Mother that God ever made. And they fell down on their knees and adored God made Man. And then Mary, with an exquisite smile of loving gratitude and motherly pride, handed them the Divine Infant to hold and to kiss.

"For us, on the contrary, both His Humanity and His Divinity are hidden. We belong to those of whom Jesus said, 'Blessed are those who have not seen and yet have believed.'

"So, no wonder then, the angels are still singing tonight what they sang for the shepherds nineteen centuries ago, and singing it for you and for me: 'Glory to God in the highest and on earth peace to men of good will.'"

No, there is no snow in Tonga on Christmas night. But there is much warmth of heart and soul-gladness, cool, crystal-clear and deep, like a shaded pool in the valley. For this is Christ's Birthday — Christ's Mass, Christmas!

CHAPTER 14

A JOKE ON FATHER THOMAS

YOU KNOW, among themselves missionaries are often like a bunch of big boys, always playing tricks on each other.

When I was sent to Haapai, that archipelago of twelve islands in the central portion of the Kingdom of Tonga, 100 miles from Tongatapu, naturally I found it quite lonesome at first.

I hadn't been used to being alone. I'd had the good fortune of serving as curate for several years with that spry little Frenchman, Father Thomas, founder of the Catholic College of Blessed Chanel in Maufanga. I missed Father Thomas' company — missed the twinkle of merriment in his eye. He had promised to write to me and he hadn't written a line. I wondered why.

Then, quite suddenly I got an idea — a wonderful idea that would make him write. I adapted

New Rectory, Lifuka, Haapai

the following yarn from a French comic book called "Le Pelerin" (The Pilgrim) and sent it to Father Thomas in the form of a newspaper:

HAAPAI GAZETTE — February 11, 1927

DEATH OF REVEREND
FATHER EMILIEN THOMAS, S.M., D.D.

Dies Smothered in His Storeroom-Bedroom

Death caused by mysterious collapse of shelves above and around his bed. Found dead as a door nail under a huge pile of cans of corned beef and fish, nails, screws, bolts, crowbars and hammers, bolts of calico, kava and yams, cases of altar wine and candles, and bags of half-rotten potatoes, etc.

Irreparable Loss of a Good Man!

Father Thomas, born in France, was always a precocious child. He had one weakness, however — Latin. A most unfortunate handicap and most mysterious too, for he was otherwise very intelligent. He wished to become a priest and a missionary, so he entered the seminary and, with the advice of his spiritual director, made up his mind to apply for a dispensation to receive Minor Orders, although he had not yet reached the canonical age.

To make up for his deficiency in Latin, he was advised to learn by heart this set of questions and answers:

1. On presenting himself before the Holy Father, he was to make a bow and say, "Salve, Sancte Pater." (Hail, Holy Father.)

2. Then the Pope would ask him, "Unde venis?" (Where do you come from?) He was to answer, "Ex Gallia" (from France).

3. The Pope would ask his age, "Quot annos habes?" (How old are you?) Young Emilian would answer, "Sexdecim" (sixteen).

4. When he was asked, "Quid vis?" (What do you want?), he was to reply, "Tonsuram et quatuor minores" (Tonsure and the four Minor Orders).

So off he went to the audience chamber. While waiting in the wonderful Vatican halls he saw so many new and marvelous things that he completely forgot his set of questions and answers.

"If I could only remember the first one, then all the rest would come back to my mind," lamented the poor boy.

Just as he was being ushered into the presence of the Pontiff, he saw an inscription beneath a beautiful Madonna. It read: "Salve, Sancta Parens" (Hail, Holy Mother).

He was delighted and thought he had found his cue. So he made a most respectful bow to the Holy Father and said in a loud, clear voice, "Salve, Sancta Parens."

The Pope was much surprised, naturally, to be saluted in this manner, and he asked, "Putas me esse mulierem?" (Do you think I am a woman?)

Emilian answered proudly, "Ex Gallia."

The startled Holy Father addressed him in a loud voice, "Demonium habes." (You have a devil in you.)

"Sexdecim," Emilian Thomas answered without batting an eyelid.

Very, very angry now at such intolerable insolence, the Pope cried out, "Quid vis?"

The young cleric began to realize that something had gone wrong. Frightened, he stuttered, "Tonsuram.... tonsuram et.... quatuor.... quatuor...." Oh, what was the last word?)

He made another effort: "Tonsuram et quatuor mulieres!" (Tonsure and four women.)

At this climax of climaxes, the Holy Father made an imperative gesture to one of his Swiss Guards, and the surprised and frightened Emilian Thomas was promptly kicked clear out the Vatican Door.

* * *

CAN YOU IMAGINE dear old Father Thomas' reaction when he read that fantastic story? Father Thomas, with the merry twinkle in his eye?

He could hardly wait to show it to the Bishop, knowing what a laugh they would have together.

"My dear Bishop, please read this letter from that young American over in Haapai! Tell me! Did you ever hear the like of it? Isn't it the limit!"

Did I get an answer? Indeed, I did! Father Thomas wrote it on pink letter paper! I forget all that he said, for that was many years ago, but I do remember that he ended with: "Si non e vero, bene trovato." (If it isn't true, it's well invented.)

And from then on we corresponded regularly. Just shows you what a well-timed and well-placed **kick** can do, doesn't it?

CHAPTER 15

STAR OF THE DEEP

WHAT'S IT LIKE to be a missionary, living alone, eighty-odd sea miles from your nearest confrere?

Well, first of all, of course, you count on prayers — the prayers of your family and friends back home in the United States; the prayers of all priests of God, especially their daily memento at Holy Mass; the prayers of all members of your religious family, Priests, Brothers, Sisters, and tertiaries; the prayers of every member of the Mystical Body of Christ. All must be missionaries through their prayers and charity.

Then too the isolated missionary counts on letters. Letters from missionary-minded friends are like sudden rays of sunshine brightening his often rugged way, encouraging him to be brave in spite of all, to spread a little further the Kingdom of God on earth, to lift a little higher the shining cross of Him, Who is the Light of the World.

What's it like to be a missionary in Lifuka Island, Haapai? Well, if you have a few moments to spare, let's imagine that you have just arrived in this little mission. Do come in and sit down. What do you think of this little room with its wide open doors and windows, its books and papers, its saws and hammers, its hats and cassocks, its old clocks awaiting repairs, its balls of twine and rolls of sailing charts, its marlin spikes and coconut-shell cups and banana leaves (cut and fried for Tongan cigarettes), its kava — kava under the bed, kava under the table, kava on that old desk salvaged from a wrecked ship, kava in the corner near the old bureau?

I can see you smile as if to say, "Well, I thought it was something like this."

What about lighting our pipes and going out for a stroll? What a beautiful day it is! The strong trade winds sway the coconut fronds to and fro, making them glint and shimmer in the golden sunlight. But you should see them in a hurricane! Plumed warriors fighting to a finish against a thundering cyclone's storm-born ramming planes!

Come across the way to the coral-sand beach. Did you ever see such a beautiful sight as this magic-colored ocean? Did you ever see such a gorgeous display as these unbelievable tints and shades of greens and blues, ever moving and changing and glittering, like a fairy sea of liquid diamonds?

There, a little further on, is our reef-protected harbor. Do you see that trim little craft with its tall mast and new rigging? And the name "Fetuu Moana" carved on the bow? That's our new mission boat, built by the natives, right here in Haapai, under the direction of the missionary. The name means "Star of the Deep." Don't you think it's an appropriate name? She's already travelled some ten thousand-odd miles these last few months, and proved herself a fine sea boat.

One night — I shall never forget it — a sudden storm hurled her bodily on the foaming edge of a cruel reef. The next morning we got her off again without a cent of damage. Do you know why? Because the "Fetuu Moana" is insured! No, not in any insurance company of this world, but in one we call "The Little Flower and Company, Unlimited."

None but the builders know the secret places in her keel and stem where we hid the many relics and medals of St. Therese. In the rudder posthead we prayerfully placed rose petals from Lisieux. (How sweet smelling they were!) In the main hatchway, just above the ship's clock, occupying the place of honor, is a picture of our Insurance Company's president, a tiny, delightfully beautiful medallion of St. Therese of the Child Jesus.

You see what precautions we had taken before launching our little boat in those reef-infested waters. But that's not all. Our auxiliary engine, a powerful Diesel motor, the first such motor ever brought to the Kingdom of Tonga, had to be insured too. Now this greasy, thundering demon would hardly have been a fit plaything to entrust to St. Therese's delicate little hands, would it? So we called on powerful St. Michael. He too belongs to the ship's company, of course. And he's been true to his task. He's made that 30 h.p. devil do some wonderful work against wind and storm. The "Fetuu Moana" leaped homeward like a snow plow on a railroad track, when no other boat was able to get through. It must have been St. Michael too who helped the missionary learn how to run the engine at all. There was no one else to teach him — unless it was St. Joseph.

You'll laugh if you take a peep down below when the missionary-engineer goes into action. You'll see his hands dirty with oil and grease, his stained shirt and khaki pants; but you'll see him smiling as he hears the motor's regular beat.

It may be rough, very rough out there many miles from land. The sea may be so bad that no meal can be prepared. But never mind. Perhaps this very evening he will land on an island where no missionary has ever been before. Perhaps tomorrow morning he will say Mass in a poor little leaf hut — the first Mass ever said on that island since time began.

So no matter how the "Fetuu Moana" tosses and plunges, no matter how hungry the missionary gets, no matter how his working clothes are drenched when he comes up on deck for a breath of fresh air, away down in his heart there is sweet melody-making and joy serene, for this is hundred-folding in Haapai. Don't you envy him?

CHAPTER 16

THE BIG BROWN DOG

WOULD YOU LIKE to hear the story of the big brown dog and how he.... But no, we mustn't let the cat out of the bag! Just imagine what the big brown dog would do to it! Well, perhaps he wouldn't chase it after all, because this particular dog has the best manners and the most sense of any dog you've ever read about.

One day the "Fetuu Moana" anchored off a beautiful palm-fronded island called Fonoi. No Catholic missionary had ever visited this island, so naturally this missionary and his "boys" felt thrilled with the spirit of adventure. As they rowed ashore they were struck by the fact that the sparkling beach was not dotted with the usual crowd of brown children, playing and swimming in the surf. Indeed, no one was to be seen. "Queer, very queer," said the priest.

Half an hour later you would have seen the baffled missionary sitting on a log in the middle

The Big Brown Dog

of a native village with its tiny, coconut-leaf huts, its broad-leafed breadfruit trees, its mango trees, its huge banyan and ironwood trees, its fish nets and rustic racks of drying octopuses, its pigs and goats and chickens.

Why were frightened children peeping through the reed walls of the houses? Why had this island forgotten the ancient laws of Tongan hospitality? Why? Because someone had solemnly warned them of the missionary's coming!

Poor Fonoi! If you only knew that the missionary whom you coldly refuse to see is Jesus Christ Who still goes from one land to another to preach the Gospel of the Kingdom! He is Jesus Christ Who carries His Cross on His shoulders through every highway of the world! "He is Jesus Christ Who goes in search of all His sheep to lead them into the fold of His Church. Jesus Christ is not dead. He lives in Heaven. He also lives and walks on earth in the person of His missionaries, diffusing His light in the darkness, pointing out the right path to the erring, giving true life to those who are dead and buried in the errors of a thousand years of paganism."

As the missionary sat there on the log, he thought of Jesus weeping over Jerusalem. And then something happened! All of a sudden, as if in answer to his thoughts, a big brown dog came rushing toward him. With yelps of glee, and wagging his bushy tail so fast that you'd wonder why it didn't drop right off, the dog went straight up to the missionary and offered him his paw.

Those big brown eyes seemed to say, "Never mind, Father. Never mind the way these folks behave. It's a shame! But let me tell you, I'll receive you here if no one else will! Come on, Father, let me show you around a bit."

From that moment the faithful big brown dog was like Mary's little lamb, following the missionary wherever he went. He even wanted to help him read his breviary, but had to content himself with sitting down and keeping quiet until the priest had finished.

The next morning the Holy Sacrifice of the Mass, the very first ever to hallow that island, was offered in a poor little hut. None of the people of Fonoi came. No one! No one but the big brown dog who came in a bit late, sat down quietly and put his nose on the knee of the captain of the "Fetuu Moana." All during Mass the animal's big brown eyes never left the little altar. He just watched all the while like a curious but very respectful human.

No one — only a dog — comes to greet Jesus! No wonder the missionary thought of Jesus in Bethlehem on that first Christmas night when the big wondering eyes of dumb beasts were the first, after Mary and Joseph, to behold God made Man.

And when the Mass was over we started to sail away from Fonoi Island, there on the glistening coral shore was the big brown dog. His bushy tail was quiet now. How sad he looked! And when at last he seemed to realize that we were really going away, he lifted his big head straight in the air and started to howl in that peculiar way dogs do when their master dies. Even when we had lost sight of him, we could still hear the mournful howling of the big brown dog, the only inhabitant of

Fonoi Island who had been glad to welcome and shake hands with the Catholic missionary, and the only one who was sorry to see him leave.

On Palm Sunday, when the high priests remonstrated with Him for allowing the children to acclaim Him, Our Lord replied, "If these should hold their peace the very stones would cry out..."

And it took the dog with the big brown eyes to greet the coming of Christ to Fonoi Island.

A poem called "The Big Black Dog" was published in an Australian magazine some years ago. With apologies to the author, Elizabeth G. Reynolds, we have adapted it to fit our brown friend of Fonoi Island:

I wonder if Christ had a big brown dog,
All curly and woolly like mine,
With the silky ears and a nose round and wet
And eyes brown and tender that shine.

I'm sure, if He had, that that big brown dog
Knew right from the first He was God,
That he needed no proofs that Christ was divine,
But just worshipped the ground that He trod.

I'm afraid that He hadn't, because I have heard
How He prayed in the garden alone,
When all of His friends and disciples had fled,
Even Peter, the one called a stone.

And oh, I am sure that the big brown dog
With a heart ever faithful and warm
Would never have left Him to suffer alone,
But creeping right under His arm,

Would have licked those dear Fingers in agony clenched,
And counting all favors but loss,
When they took Him away, would have trotted behind
And followed Him quite to the Cross!

CHAPTER 17

HE THREW A BOOK
AT HIS MOTHER-IN-LAW

DID I MEET any extraordinary characters in those thirty years I was in Tonga? Why, of course I did! The place is full of them.

One of the most extraordinary was dear old Litea (pronounced Lee-tay-ah, with accent on the second syllable). The fact that she was super-extraordinary will immediately strike you the minute I tell you that her conversion began in that split second when her son-in-law threw the book at her. "The Lives of the Saints," I mean.

You see, she was a good Wesleyan angel — hat, red shawl and all. (When the Wesleyans of Tonga name a woman an angel, on account of her regular attendance at church, she receives the right to wear a hat in church. Catholic women there don't wear hats.) She was a good Wesleyan angel and she just didn't like Catholics. Not even when they happened to be sons-in-law.

Throwing a book at someone, by the way, doesn't seem so bad when you've lived in Tonga for a while, because in the Land of Upside Down that's the way they often hand you things. They just throw them at you. The altar boys do it in the sanctuary. People do it at meal times. So you really have to get used to catching things and catching them in the right way, or else!

Well, anyhow, Litea took one look at the title of the book, "Kau Sangato" (Lives of the Saints), and grunted her disgust by that one very little but very strong Tongan word, "VI!" (pronounced vee) — "VI!" After all, wasn't she more than eighty years old? For several years now she hadn't been able to get around the village or even go to church and they couldn't expect her to change her ways at this point, could they? What was this so-and-so son-in-law thinking about? He had married her favorite daughter, Vai Sini (Gin Water), who had become a Catholic. Was he insinuating?

But she didn't have a chance to tell him what she thought of him. Right after the book-throwing act the young man had quickly departed, going while the going was good. Curiosity got the best of her, however, and despite her "VI!s" of disgust, Litea couldn't resist opening the book. After all it wouldn't bite her. If it offended her she could always drop it like a hot potato or, better still, throw it back at him when he'd come, as he surely would, to borrow a chew of tobacco. So she adjusted her ancient spectacles, fastened to her ears by bits of wire and string, and started to read.

Let's take a peep at her as she reads. She's sitting on a mat on the floor, in a large oval-shaped Tongan house with reed walls. The house has no windows, just four wide-open doors that let in the bright sunshine and fresh air. They also let in quite a few hens and roosters that strut around quietly looking for stray bits of food on the mat-covered floor. A contented cat is taking a nap on the sunny doorsill. The huge tie-beams of the roof structure are well weighted down with great rolls of tapa cloth and big bundles of mats, showing how thrifty Litea has been all through the years.

Notice how white she is, almost like a European. Her face is decidedly not Polynesian, for it is rather oval-shaped. Her nose is thin and aquiline. Her mouth, when closed, denotes firmness and will power. When open, it seems a bit large and her square-shaped teeth have spaces between them, but few of them are missing. Her smile kindles an almost roguish gleam of joy in her dark brown, deep-sunken eyes. She is tall, thin and wiry, with long arms and legs that look very old compared to her smooth, almost wrinkleless face. Her snow-white hair is neatly combed and parted in the middle, then tied in a knot on the back of her head. Seventy years ago she must have been a pretty girl and a lively one too. She still is.

See how attentive she is to her reading. She has become deeply interested. Those slow, very slow motions of her head indicate her approval and surprise and genuine admiration. Never has she read anything so beautiful in all her long life. A freak ray of sunshine breaks through a little chink in the coconut-leaf roof and makes sparkling, liquid diamonds of the tears that fill Litea's eyes.

Something similar is happening in her soul. Old Litea hadn't been an angel for nothing. She knew her Bible. She remembered that only "the good tree produces good fruit." A religion that could produce men and women like these "sangato" must be — couldn't be anything else than the true Church Christ Himself had founded. It was as simple as that to her! Before she was halfway through the book, God had given her the gift of faith. Not long afterward she was baptized and, needless to say, the man whom God had inspired to throw the book at her became her favorite son-in-law.

Another remarkable thing happened too. Within a short time after her conversion she grew strong again. As she regained her health, she was able to go out on the reef with the other women of the village and collect sea food in her basket, as is the daily custom at low-tide all over Oceania.

She owned a plantation in the bush and now

she could go there again too, and bring home coconuts and vegetables. Everyone was astounded to see her moving around like a "fine mui" (fee-ney moo-y — a young woman). She would just smile at their surprise and tell them, "You become a Catholic, too."

She herself was an exemplary one, of course. She learned her morning and evening prayers right away. And she fell deeply in love with Our Lady of Lourdes, Patroness of the little chapel on Uiha Island where Litea lived.

The last time I saw Litea in good health was on the day she attended the "Fononga Tapu" (Corpus Christi procession) at Lifuka. The Catholic Mission Center at Lifuka is the only place in the Haapai archipelago where the Blessed Sacrament is kept regularly. On the feasts of Corpus Christi and Christmas, as well as during Holy Week, all Catholics from the other islands are brought to the Mission Center and taken home again afterward — a big job, as you may imagine. The celebration of Corpus Christi lasts all day, beginning with Mass in the morning and ending with a magnificent procession in the afternoon. Four Altars of Repose are arranged outdoors, one on each of the four corners of the concourse around which the procession moves.

Litea had come from her home in Uiha, ten miles away, for Corpus Christi. She was so happy to be doing something special for Our Lord in the Most Blessed Sacrament. She spent hours in the church adoring Him and visiting with Him in her own childlike way, kneeling all the time on the cold, bare cement floor, without even a mat under her knees.

I asked her, "Why don't you go over there and kneel where there is a mat?"

She answered simply with a smile, as much as to say, "Thank you, Father, but I'm offering this up in a spirit of penance." And remember, she was then about eighty-five years old!

Well, when Corpus Christi Day was over she went back to Uiha, her island, and the next night it happened. She took her two grandchildren, a little boy and girl, with her to her plantation. They were to spend the night there where she had a little hut, a makeshift shelter built of coconut leaves. The Tongans often leave a light burning all night because they are, even now, very superstitious and afraid of such things as ghosts and burial grounds.

During the night the night-light fell over and set the hut on fire. The coconut leaves were so dry that the little shelter was soon burning furiously. The boy was the first to feel the heat. He woke up his grandmother and they both dashed instinctively out of the fire. Then, fully awake at last, Litea remembered her little "mokopuna" (granddaughter) and, without the slightest hesitation, went back into that inferno, crawling on her hands and knees. She brought the little girl out safe and sound, but Litea herself was critically burned.

When I saw her a few hours later her poor old body was as black as coal all over, except for her chest where she had clasped the little girl close to her bosom. Her back was horribly burned. They had put her on a bed of green banana leaves where, in great agony, she awaited my arrival.

When she saw the priest coming with the Blessed Sacrament, she seemed to forget all her pain and greeted her God and the man who brought Him with a heavenly smile of welcome. The deep reverence and adoration and loving gratitude with which she received the Last Sacraments were edifying to see.

Then the T.M.P. (Tongan doctor) arrived and ordered her to be taken to the hospital on Lifuka Island. But it was already nightfall, so we had to wait until dawn. The next day was Sunday, so I planned to say my first Mass here in Uiha and my second in Lifuka, accompanying the poor old lady on the mission launch.

Just as I was finishing my early Mass I noticed the natives entering the main gate leading to our chapel, carrying Litea on a mat. She was just in time to hear the catechist intone the final hymn to the Blessed Mother. She asked her friends to let her rest on the grass in front of the chapel.

From there she could clearly see the statue of her beloved Lady of Lourdes. Just as the last verse of the hymn, a beautiful commentary on Our Lady's "Memorare," was being sung, old Litea expired with an exquisite smile of ecstatic happiness on her face. Our Lady of Lourdes had taken her home.

I sailed back to Lifuka for the High Mass at 8 o'clock and that same afternoon sailed back to Uiha for Litea's burial, taking with me the Sisters, convent girls, the Brass Band and other Catholics — two boat-loads of them. We all returned to Lifuka that evening after a hectic day's work for the Lord.

Litea was buried about 4 o'clock that afternoon. The text of the sermon was easy to find for everyone was thinking, "Greater love than this no man has, that a man lay down his life for his friends."

Litea had entered the Catholic Church through the lives of the saints. In His infinite wisdom and goodness, God arranged that she should enter the celestial abode of those same saints, perhaps directly and immediately, with no delay in purgatory, for wasn't she a martyr of charity?

So, all in all, isn't it remarkable what can come from such a combination of innocent looking circumstances as having a book thrown at you, attending a Corpus Christi procession and being afraid of ghosts? "All things work together unto good for them that love the Lord."

CHAPTER 18

OLD MAN KEROSENE

EVERYBODY LOVED old man Kerosene. His full name was Fehoko Kalasini Tukimomoko, which means Fehoko Kerosene, the Cold-Metal-Blacksmith.

Yes, Fehoko Kerosene, the Cold-Metal-Blacksmith, must have been the most popular old man on the whole island. Everyone loved him — loved his big, broad smile, his tall tales, his wise cracks and his jokes which, I must admit, were not always of the drawing room variety.

They used to kid him about the Samoan tatoo on his body. It pictured a sort of skin-deep, very elaborate pair of tights, all tattooed in the best technicolor by some first-class Samoan tattooer.

And everybody admired his huge, strong hands which, in spite of his age, were still young and vigorous and contrasted sharply with the rest of his shrivelled-up old body. "His body is old," they said, "but his heart and hands are still young."

So one day when it became known that Kerosene's fat, renegade son had beaten up his poor old dad, everybody was very angry. In one of our Sunday morning, after-Mass kava parties, it was decided that we would all get together and build our old friend a nice little Tongan hut right here near the Patele's own house, and invite him to come live there for the rest of his days.

How gladly he accepted this invitation! Here he was happy as could be. He kept singing away all day long as he busied himself beating out big six-inch nails on his old anvil, making knives of them. That's why he was called Tukimomoko, which literally means "beating out iron without preheating it."

Perhaps you wonder what he did with all those knives. He would barter them for all kinds of things — for tobacco, for eggs, for fish, for fruit — or he would simply use them as presents to those who did his scant washing and mending or other favors.

But he specialized in cats. How he did love cats! I mean how he did love to **eat them**! It was really marvelous to see how, in spite of his seventy-odd years, he was such a good marksman with a slingshot. Many a cat lost its whole nine lives right there near old Kalasini's little brown hut. Whenever I heard a joyous war whoop coming from that direction I knew that it meant one more cat for the old man's boiling pot. One cat would last him about three days — unless he invited other folks to dinner.

Where did he get the name Kerosene? Well, to tell you the truth, in all the years he lived with me, I never thought of asking him. You see, we are so used to peculiar names in Tonga. There are indeed some amusing ones. Nor are they always very poetical or even very fit to translate into English. Here are a few chosen at random: Manu (animal); Latiume (radium); Te Moa (hen manure); Kuli Tea (white dog); Motua Puaka (old pig); Nimonia (pneumonia); Makoni (Marconi); Letio (radio); Mosa'ati (Mozart); Fieota'anga (one who loves to eat raw shark meat), etc.

There are also "living calendar names." These are given to commemorate some important or interesting event, such as: Senituli (century); Laui Kuonga (forever and ever); Foki Mei Amelika (back from America).

This last name was bestowed in my honor. Shortly after my return from America in 1932 a little boy was born and he was given this name. Another baby born about the same time was called Olioni, the Tongan version of the name of the boat I had sailed on, the Orion.

When the town clock was installed in the church tower a little boy was called Uasi (town clock). If anyone ever wanted to know when this clock was installed, he would be told, "You know that young man, Uasi? Well, the clock was put in the tower when he was born."

If someone asked, "When did Patele come back from America?" people would say, "Do you know so-and-so's son who is called Foki Mei Amelika? Well, it was when this boy was born."

That's what we mean by the expression "living calendar names." They can be very useful, as you see.

One of the most fantastic names you ever could imagine was given in the following circumstances. A certain good lady was always losing all her babies at birth. Then a new T.M.P. came along. (T.M.P. means Tongan Medical Practitioner — a young man trained in the Fiji Native Medical School.) When the lady's time had arrived for another baby, this efficient young T.M.P. attended her and succeeded in saving the life of her child. The parents were so overjoyed that they asked him to choose the infant's name, and he did — Veni Vidi Vici. I wonder what old Caesar would think of that?

Well now, let's get back to our old Fehoko Kalasini Tukimomoko. One day as I was rummaging through my trunk I found something which I immediately decided to give to my old friend — something which made him very, very happy indeed, even happier than when he had shot and eaten some stray cat.

You would never guess what it was, so I will tell you. A brand new fleece-lined unionsuit. He was so tickled with it when I presented it to him that he put it on the top of his head and, holding it with his two big hands, he made a nice bow, saying at the same time, an ear-to-ear smile on his face, "Patele, malo aupito, aupito, malo e ofa!" (Father, thank you very, very much and thanks so much for your great love!)

The next Sunday morning, just as I was going out into the sanctuary for the Asperges (blessing with holy water), I noticed that all the Sisters were in the act of dashing out of church by a side door and all of them simply choking with laughter. I just wondered what had happened. But I didn't have to wonder long.

As I was going down the central aisle, blessing the people with holy water, I nearly dropped dead when, to my great surprise and horror, I beheld my old Kerosene, standing as straight as an arrow, proud as a peacock, and wearing **only** that unionsuit I had given him. It was a bit baggy in places, for it was evidently oversize and, to make matters worse, it was easy to see that the "back door" was not too well closed. He hadn't yet mastered that master button. Yet there he was, serene and happy, wearing nothing but his skin-deep tattooed tights and that unionsuit!

Old Kerosene in his...unionsuit!

Men like Thomas Gray have said, "Where ignorance is bliss 'tis folly to be wise." But just the same, I would like to have seen Mr. Thomas Gray in my place. It was one of those very embarrassing zero hours in a missionary's life, when he feels like exploding with laughter and yet, on account of the time and the place, he knows that he musn't. So I strove and struggled to keep a serious face and concentrated on giving old Kerosene an extra dose of holy water.

After Mass I called the old peacock over to the sacristy door and did my best to explain to him why we didn't want him to come to church rigged up that way again. At this anticlimax, he was simply dumbfounded. His good old face got so criss-crossed with exclamation points and question marks that it looked for all the world like a living jig-saw puzzle.

Talk about a super-flabbergasted gentleman!

"Father, my dear Father.....what is.....the matter, anyhow? After all, ain't I dressed up from head to foot?"

What could you do with a man like that? To make it clearer to him what was meant by undergarments in general and underwear in particular, and to save him any further mental hopscotch, I gave him my old (and only) bathrobe to wear over his unionsuit.

"Ain't I glad I'm dressed up for the occasion!"

Then like the sun bursting through a dark cloud, his old face fairly beamed with delight. For now, **now,** he was sure to be the best dressed man in the whole parish!

Too bad you didn't see him at Mass the following Sunday. He was so exquisitely happy, attired in that old bathrobe worn over his unionsuit, that he seemed to be floating on a pink cloud somewhere around the top of Mount Thabor with Moses and Elias and St. Peter. Certainly he appeared to be thinking, "Lord, isn't it good for us to be here! And ain't I glad I'm so well dressed up for The Occasion!"

CHAPTER 19

ESTHER AND THE FOOLISH DEVIL

YOU SHOULD HAVE SEEN little Esther at the supreme moment of her first meeting with our Lord at the Communion table. Her face was transfigured by sheer joy and gladness and radiant with simple childlike love and faith. It had cost her so much to be able to reach Him at last. And Jesus was happy to make her realize, in His own divine way, that all the trouble she had gone through for His love's sake was infinitely worth while.

She was about thirteen years old the first time I met her. I had finished saying Mass on a little island of the Haapai group and was starting to pack the Mass kit, when I heard a light cough behind me. Turning around I saw the little girl sitting on the mat-covered floor.

"Malo e lelei, kii taahine." (Good morning, little girl.)

"Malo e lelei, Patele." (Good morning, Father.)

"Koeha ae mea oku ke fie mau?" (Is there anything I can do for you?)

Her big brown eyes got bigger still and a slight blush appeared on her cheeks. It was easy to see that she was embarrassed. She had something to say and couldn't find the right words. Finally she managed to speak, "Patele, this is the first time I ever came to your lotu (church) and I love it. I don't know how to say it but, when you lifted up the little round white Thing and the shining golden cup, while the boy rang the little bell and everybody bowed their heads, I felt that God was right here in this little hut."

"And so He was, my little girl. So He was!"

Oh, the marvels of grace I have witnessed among the simple people of the islands! Their simplicity, their ready faith, win blessings for them that are incredible to the intellectual pride of more "enlightened" nations. Truly, God hides His secrets from the worldly wise and reveals them to little ones — like Esther. No natural intuition made her guess the magnificent truth of His hidden but real Presence.

"Oh, Patele," she cried, "tell me more about this wonderful thing!"

I explained to her briefly the doctrine of the Blessed Eucharist and the Sacrifice of the Mass.

She was simply thrilled. Her big brown eyes shone with an eagerness-to-know and a sudden gleam of understanding.

She put her whole soul into her next words: "Patele, may I become a Catholic? May I too receive Him like the other people did this morning?"

"Of course," I told her, "but first you must learn this little book by heart." And I gave her a tiny pink-covered catechism, showing her how much to learn before my next visit the following month.

She told me that her name was Esther (Esita, in Tongan), that her father and mother were dead and that she was living in her brother's house with her aunts.

When I returned a month later I wondered why I didn't see her at Mass. Then I got a hunch. So after breakfast (bread-fruit, coffee and nice big, fried fish eyes) I went over to Esther's home and it didn't take me long to see that my hunch was right.

Standing in the doorway and blocking the entrance stood several old women who reminded me of witches. Most of them were toothless, their hair undone and their dresses most untidy. They glared and glared and stared and stared, until I couldn't help thinking the Devil himself was in them all. I even imagined a whiff of sulphur in the air.

The hate-filled silence was shattered at last by a high-pitched, shaky old voice crying, "The girl you're looking for is ill. We can take care of her ourselves. We don't need you."

Yes, my hunch was right! And now that I had come, I had to see Esther. So, ignoring their protests and insults, I walked through the group of women and into the house. There was Esther, lying on her back in the middle of the room, crying her heart out. She was almost naked and some sort of Tongan remedy, made of a greenish, oily paste mixed with shiney leaves, was smeared on her stomach. Another group of women, as unkempt as the first, surrounded her. They were disturbed and distressed at my sudden unwelcome appearance. One of them said, "This little girl has a devil in her tummy and we are going to take it out."

A sudden tingle of anger ran up my spine and burst into a fireworks of words that cut like a whip. "No! You're all wrong! Every one of you! This little girl has no devil inside her but she has an awful lot of them around her! Now get out of the way!"

The surprised women retreated to a corner of the house and I went up to the poor little girl and knelt beside her. With sobs and tears she told me how angry they all were because she had gone to Mass and wanted to become a Catholic. Anything but that! Her aunts were all furious. Her whole family was disgusted and angry with her.

I tried to console her. "Esther, be of good heart. This is not the first time the Devil has ever kicked up a row against God. But every time he does, God wins out in the end. Don't feel bitter toward your aunts and the rest of your family. They don't know any better. It's not really their fault. Some day they'll be glad that you became a Catholic. Now before I leave I'll give you a big blessing. So cheer up. You'll see. God will clear away all the obstacles from your path, in His own way and His own time. Maybe — who knows? — you'll be able to become a Catholic and receive Him in Holy Communion much sooner than you dare hope."

That night Esther's relatives held a family meeting. "She must be taken away from the influence of the Catholic missionary," they agreed. So they decided to send her to an island eighteen miles away, that belonged to her brother, and leave her there to feed the pigs and chickens which were the only other living inhabitants of the lonely place.

Before sailing Esther was careful to hide her little catechism in her dress. When they returned home and left her there all alone in that island, they must have wondered why she didn't seem to mind at all. In fact, she seemed almost glad. Now she had a wonderful chance to study her catechism to her heart's content.

See how foolish the Devil can be? He had prompted her relatives to a decision which proved to be exactly what Esther needed most — the chance to learn all that was necessary, in order to become a Catholic and receive her First Communion.

I asked her afterward, "Esther, weren't you afraid to be left all alone like that?"

She seemed surprised that I should ask such a question. Without a second's hesitation, she replied, "Father, you know I was never alone. Doesn't the little catechism say, 'God is everywhere'? I wasn't alone a single minute of the day or night, Father. I was with God and God was with me. Of course I couldn't see Him but He could see me."

After a few weeks she had learned her catechism from cover to cover and knew all the prayers by heart. (Tongans have wonderful memories.) So she said to herself, "Now I must go to the place where Patele lives and ask him to baptize me and let me receive Holy Communion."

Lifuka, where Patele lived, was fifty-eight sea miles away. How could she ever get there? Like all island girls, Esther knew how to do many things and in spite of her extreme youth she was thrifty and ingenious. She gathered a pile of dry wood for a big bonfire, and kept some live coals handy so she could light her bonfire in a jiffy. Then she stayed on the beach every day, looking for a boat from the south. She knew that was the direction the inter-island sailboats came from.

One day she spied a tiny speck of white on the distant southern rim of the sky. A sail! Her brave little heart thumped faster and faster with joy as she got down on her hands and knees and started to blow for all she was worth, so that those live coals would get her big bonfire going quickly. She wanted to make a smoke signal to that boat. She knew how too, because she had helped grown-up folks do it many times, just because it was so much fun. She also knew it was an unwritten law in this part of the world that, when you wished to hail a passing ship for some important reason, all you had to do was make a smoke signal — a bright bonfire upon which you then put green branches and green leaves, so the smoke would become black and could be seen for many miles.

That's what little Esther did. Soon she noticed, to her great delight, that her signal had been seen. The boat had altered its course and was heading straight for her island.

Would the captain believe her story? Would he consent to take her to where Patele lived? Was it wrong for her to run away like this? These and many other such questions must have buzzed through her young mind as the fast little sail boat sped nearer and nearer.

The captain, although not a Catholic, proved to be a friend of the Catholic missionary. When he heard the little girl's story he was angry at her relatives. "Do you mean to say they put you on this island to feed the pigs and left you here all by yourself? Weren't you afraid?"

When she showed him her little pink-covered treasure and told him, "It says God is everywhere. I wasn't alone," the rough old seaman said in a husky voice, "And you want me to take you to the Patele's place?"

"Yes, please do," she pleaded.

"I certainly will," he agreed. "Come now. Jump up on my back and I'll take you aboard the ship right now."

To his men, who had been picking green coconuts for drinking, he cried, "Come on, everybody. Stop toliniu (picking coconuts). Come now. All aboard for Lifuka, Haapai."

That evening about nightfall Esther came running into my house, her hair undone and her dress untidy, but her beautiful eyes sparkling. All in one breath she cried out, "Patele, I ran away from my brother's island. I know my little catechism from beginning to end. May I be baptized and receive Holy Communion?"

"Wonderful! Wonderful!" I exclaimed. "But hold on a bit. We can't go too fast. You'll have to stay here in the convent school a little while."

Esther and the foolish Devil

"But, Patele, this is the only dress I have. I have no bed, no box, nothing." She started to cry and said, "My aunts will come and get me and make me go back with them. They'll give me a terrible beating for running away like this. They'll say I have another devil in my tummy."

"No, they won't," I promised her, knowing that in spite of their intense opposition to the Catholic Church the people all had great respect for our Mission Compounds, a respect that amounted to a healthy fear, so they would not dare come there to get the child against the wish of the priest.

"Now don't cry," I told her. "You're a big girl now. Here comes Mother Superior. She'll take care of you from now on, won't you Sister?"

"Of course we will, Father," the nun assured us both. "Come, Esther. Don't worry any more. We'll give you all you need."

When the other girls in the convent school heard Esther's story they were happy to share their mats and dresses and towels and soap and everything she needed. They all admired this little girl's spunk and the wonderful way God had brought her to their school. She was such a simple child, so unpretentious and yet so brave, that she soon won everybody's heart.

When First Communion Day came the following June, and the Patele prepared the children for this big occasion by a three-day retreat, you can guess who knew her lessons best, who was the most attentive to the instructions and who had the sweetest look of peace and happiness on her face.

No, that's not the end of the story of the little run-away girl and her bitter foe, the Devil. The end of the story hasn't yet been written. You can help write it — by praying for Esther. You've probably known similar true stories to happen among your own relatives and friends. You may have played a leading role in such a story yourself.

The Devil doesn't give up easily. In some souls he seems to take a particularly violent interest. Perhaps in some mysterious way they are — and he knows it — extraordinary precious prey. Perhaps, in the unfathomable designs of Divine Providence, their very falls from grace are destined, in the end, to prove among those "felices culpae" (happy faults) that only serve to point up, for all who have eyes to see, the magnificent mercy of the Redeemer who triumphs at the last.

"Be of good heart, Esther. This is not the first time the Devil has ever kicked up a row against God. But every time he does, God wins out in the end."

Esther remained in the convent until she was firmly grounded in the Faith. Then she went back to her home and was faithful for a long time. But she got "marriage fever" and married outside the Church — most unhappily too, for her husband would beat her whenever she tried to go to the Catholic Church. Gradually she gave up. The poor child got tired of beatings. And then "the hand of the Lord touched her" with a pitiful affliction, no doubt for His own wise reasons.

The last time I saw her she smiled through a rainbow of tears — poor thing! One must pray for her. She may not be guilty at all, perhaps, before God, Who is so understanding and forgiving. He hasn't given up hope. He is such an optimist. So pray for Esther sometimes — for the little girl who was so wonderful when she was small, and turned out so pathetically when she grew up. Let us hope she'll run away one last time — and this time into the Hands of her Father in Heaven, who is still watching the road, just as He did long ago for the prodigal son.

CHAPTER 20

PANGO AND THE SHARK

SHOULD YOU EVER GO to Tonga (and I hope you do) be sure to go over to the Island of Nomuka and get Pango, the Catholic Mission catechist, to tell you his own story. But you'd better go soon for Pango is getting old and preparing humbly to go home to God to thank Him in person for all the graces of a long lifetime, as catechist, as father of thirteen children, most of whom are happily married, and for having stopped that big man-eating shark just in the nick of time.

The Island of Nomuka was well known in the days of sailing ships, as it was one of the few places in this part of the vast South Pacific Ocean where there is a fresh water lake. That's why Captain Bligh's men of the ill-fated BOUNTY went ashore there. Did you ever hear of "The Mutiny on the Bounty"? Well, this is where it started. But that's

Pango and his wife "Lola"

another story. This one is about Pango and the shark, the terrifying, dreaded "tenifa," a 15-foot brute, dull brown in color.

It was a bright summer morning and the lively, brown-skinned, black-eyed kiddies of Nomuka Island were running about and playing on the snow-white beach. See how the coral sand sparkles. See how crystal-clear the water is, with its flower beds of varicolored coral plants growing on the sandy bottom of the bay. Look over there a few yards beyond the high-water mark and notice how the grown-ups are enjoying the cool, breeze-swept shade of that gorgeous banyan or "ovava" tree, smoking, chatting and day-dreaming the time away in this happy, carefree land.

PANGO AND THE SHARK

Along the patch leading down from the village strolled a tall, wiry native carrying a knife in his hand, a big roll of fish line on his arm and a long pole on his shoulder. He walked straight to his small outrigger canoe and pulled it from the sandbank into the sea.

"Alu kife?" (Where are you going?) someone shouted from the shade of the ovava tree.

"Taumanga" (fishing for snappers), answered Pango. This "manga" (snapper) is a red, flat fish that loves deep water, fifty fathoms or more.

Little did Pango realize that he was pulling that canoe of his into the sea for the last time. Nor could those simple folks on shore ever imagine what a wonderful topic of conversation they would have before night, what a red-hot story would buzz around the village and hit the headlines of that South Sea substitute for the daily newspaper, the ever popular kava party. Between big bowls of cool, non-intoxicating kava, and through thick clouds of strong smelling Tongan tobacco, they would re-enact the drama and, with thrilled amazement and shaking of heads, they would wonder how in the world that big tenifa, that huge man-eating shark ever could or would.....

But hold on! Wait a minute! We are anticipating. We are going too fast. Nothing has happened yet. Pango is just quietly paddling out to sea. Notice how the broad blade of his home-made paddle glistens in the sunlight at every stroke. How indigo blue the water is. How calm the sea. Ideal weather, this, for snapper fishing.

When he reached a spot about five miles from shore — about five miles beyond the thundering reef — he played out his line with its triple hooks all baited and ready, and started fishing. Here the water was beautifully colored in all imaginable tints of green and blue coral, ever changing in the glittering rays of the tropical sun, then suddenly sparkling into a fringe of liquid pearl and dazzling diamond.

There in the tiny canoe, Pango, the catechist, with his tattooed body dressed only in a bit of loin cloth around his middle and a huge scapular medal around his neck, was calmly fishing with a length of fish line and home-made hooks. He had a large family to feed, so he was anxious to catch all the fish he could. They were awaiting his arrival before they ate the first of their two meals for the day.

For about an hour he had very good luck. If anyone had been around, he could have heard the glad cry of the lucky Tongan fisherman, "Kai tolu!" (triple catch!), and would have seen him, not once but several times, pull up his line with a nice, big, wriggling snapper on each of the three hooks.

And then it happened! Suddenly and without warning, for all the world like the silent surfacing of a submarine, a big, dull brown tenifa came up from the deep, right close to Pango's little boat — a giant, slimy back, with pointed fins. My, what a big fellow he was! Much longer than Pango's canoe. How wickedly those yellowish green shark-eyes glittered with greed as they looked over such promising prospects for a good meal.

But Pango had a different idea. If only he had brought his spear! "Oh, why did I leave it home?" he muttered. All he had was a knife and a long pole. Quickly he sharpened the pole with the knife. If he could just pierce one of those devilish looking eyes, what a banquet his wife and children would have, and all the neighbors too.

He stood up cautiously, took careful aim, and VRING! — down went the improvised spear with terrific force. But the sudden jerk on the little craft caused him slightly to miss his shot and, instead of hitting the wicked eyeball, his spear struck the edge of the eye socket, a bone hard as flint and glanced off into the sea. The startled shark disappeared into the depths below. Pango recovered his spear and, all poised in readiness, waited for another chance.

He waited and waited but the crafty shark didn't seem to want to come back at all. So Pango started fishing again. Then, as if that was just what the big brute had been waiting for, all of a sudden the water was seething beneath his little boat. With an unearthly bellow, the huge shark struck the keel of the canoe a torpedo-like blow and broke it into smithereens. Pango was hurled high in the air and fell into the foaming sea, just in time to see the big tenifa race off at a terrific pace with a chunk of the outrigger float-log in his gleaming teeth.

The shark must have noticed pretty soon that it didn't taste too good and that he had mistaken a piece of wood for a man's leg for, after a few hundred yards, he suddenly spun around, quick as lightning, and sped back toward the poor native like a live rocket. The spray he made on the surface of the sea was like white steam.

Pango, of course, well realized his danger, as he tried frantically to swim away from the terrible monster. He was five miles from shore. No other boat was in sight. No one could help him now. No one could ever hear him. No one, that is, but God — God, Who is everywhere. Pango knew that too. So he cried out with all his might — with all the strength of his loving faith, "Lord, Lord Jesus, save me! Mother of God, help me, help me quick!"

Only a few yards from his victim the voracious shark suddenly and abruptly stopped dead in his tracks, just as though he had struck a stone wall. He paused. He seemed puzzled. And then....

But let Pango tell it, just as he told me two days later when I happened into Nomuka on a rou-

Pango — Shark Story

tine monthly visit. I found him reclining on a mat, his head resting on his wooden pillow. He was still quite exhausted after his terrible ordeal. I noticed a few scratches on his bare chest and legs and asked him the reason for them. He told me the story.

"Patele," he said, "I thought my last day had come. I shuddered as I thought of being torn to pieces and eaten alive there in the deep with no one to help me. I prayed as I never prayed before. Only God could help me, since only He could see me. Three times I said, 'Sacred Heart of Jesus, have mercy on me. St. Therese of the Child Jesus, help! help! help!'

"And the huge shark, tearing toward me at a terrific speed, suddenly slowed down and, just as if someone was forcing him under the water, he disappeared quietly and slowly into the deep. And he didn't come up again. I was filled with a strange strength as I swam back to shore. I knew God had heard my prayer."

Did I believe Pango's story? I certainly did! There are skeptics in America who won't. People who scoff at miracles and shake their heads in haughty indifference and stubborn doubt. As though God Who made the laws of nature can't, if He so wills, make an exception to these laws! People who refuse to believe that prayer and faith are the most powerful forces in the world. Give me the simple, strong faith of my natives who turn to God in loving, childlike confidence and experience His prompt response!

After listening to Pango's story, I asked him, "How long did it take you to swim back to shore, Pango?"

"I don't know, Patele," he replied. "It must have taken several hours. There's a bad current, you know."

"And weren't you afraid the shark might come back after you?"

"No, Patele," he said. "I wasn't a bit afraid. I knew God was watching over me."

Then the good man started to weep. "Patele, excuse me for crying like this. I can't help it when I think how God has been so merciful to hear the prayer of a poor man like me. No one could help me. No one could hear me — no one but God alone. But He heard me! Oh, the wonderful goodness of God! He saved me from the shark!"

I felt the warm tears on my own cheeks too, and remembered the words of Tennyson:

"More things are wrought by prayer than this world dreams of."

So when you go to Tonga, and it had better be soon, go over to Nomuka and let Pango tell you his story all over again.

CHAPTER 21

THE GHOST WAS MISBEHAVIN'

.....SO THEY SHOT HIM three times! He was a prominent cricket player of Nomuka. He was very popular. The people buried him deep.....

Burial customs in Tonga are strange to Americans. You see, the Tongan regards his dead with a mixture of devotion, respect and superstition. If you saw one of their graveyards you would be astounded. It looks like a field of beautiful white sand covered with huge birthday cakes. They allow nothing to grow there because they've got it in the back of their heads that, if the root of a tree or plant were to penetrate the body of a dead relative, those still living would develop a pain in the corresponding part of their bodies. And there's nothing you can say to dissuade them either! (I mean, of course, the uneducated ones.)

To them, it would be a sacrilege to bury a person in firm soil. The graveyards are always on the beach or at least in sandy soil. In the latter case, as much soil as possible is dug out and the grave is filled in with pure, white sand. This is done after the sermon. The priest preaches at every burial if he can. It's the only time he can guarantee having the whole population present.

Immediately after the sermon is finished the chief man of the bereaved family makes the "tuutunis," which means the regulations for that particular funeral. The place, the time, the kind of banquet, all are settled then, and that's the real reason why you can always be sure of having the whole population present. No Tongan will ever miss an opportunity for a banquet, unless he is feeling sick unto death himself!

As soon as the body is put in the grave the relatives bring baskets of different kinds of sand. Coarse sand goes in first, then slightly finer sand, and finally, on top, the finest sand they can find. Then they take all the different kinds of coral and pebbles from a volcano (there are two volcanos in our district), shine them with coconut oil and arrange them in special designs. It all looks very, very nice.

The depth of the grave varies, those who were much loved being buried deep while a poor person who wasn't particularly well liked is put in a shallow grave. Well, anyway, the chap we started to tell you about was buried deep, and they even provided a conk-shell "band" for the occasion. After six months, however, he began walking around the village at night, disturbing everyone — so those claimed who said they saw him. One of my best Catholics, Manu (a name which means "animal"), swore that he had come into her room the night before! The chiefs of the village took exception to these antics. They dug up the poor corpse and shot him in public three times, with a shotgun. They reburied him and he never walked again.

Sometimes, when a relative who has been dead for many years "appears" in a dream, the people go out and exhume his remains. They move the bones around to confuse the ghost, thinking he'll be so mixed up he can't walk any more. Then they go back home and hope for the best.

The ordinary native is buried in tapa and mats. The higher his rank the more mats there will be. A mat has high value in the islands. The poor people, on the other hand, are buried in caskets. And that's where I come in. We've made many a casket in our workshop. In Tonga, a casket consists simply of six boards, a bit of cloth and no handles. The people insist on nailing down the cover. I used to make screw-holes for them, but they couldn't see the point. They would just place a nail in another part of the wood, next to the hole, and hammer it down. Of course I soon learned better and forgot all about such advanced ideas as screws.

One woman tried out her casket in advance, to make sure it would fit. This was rather an exceptional case. She was a very sick woman. They were making the casket in the next room and when they had finished she asked them to bring it in so she could take a look at it. "A good job," she commented. "Now let me try it out." She did, and was delighted with the fit. The next day she died! And at the burial were they proud of her feat of the previous day!

It is difficult to give a completely Catholic burial. Their traditions are so different and, as with any other nation, a burial is a sacred thing. However, we do the best we can and, while we give them all the ceremonies the Church can provide, we try also to follow their customs as much as possible. The result is quite impressive.

CHAPTER 22

GOD AND TONGA ARE MY HERITAGE

TIME IS SUCH a tricky prism. It seems only yesterday that I had the unforgettable thrill of meeting Her Majesty, Queen Salote, for the first time. Actually it was a good twenty years ago. She had come to Haapai for the first time in several years — her first visit since I had been in charge of the Catholic Mission in that twelve-island archipelago.

It was a bright sunny morning in 1932 when all the Catholic people of Lifuka came in a body to pay grateful homage and respect to their Queen, at the nice old wooden house which is always her headquarters when she visits in Lifuka. Leading the procession was our Brass Band. Then came the smiling convent girls, their legs, arms and faces shining with scented coconut oil. The Sisters followed, accompanied by the other Catholic women, and bringing the Queen a beautifully decorated cake, as well as gifts of mats, fans etc.; and finally the men, attired in their Sunday best and the traditional and distinctive Tongan tao vala (ceremonial mat) worn over the ordinary loincloth as a mark of respect.

By the time I arrived at the Queen's house, the Sisters and their girls and many of the other women were sitting on the floor of the large veranda which surrounds three sides of the house, all as close as they could get to Her Majesty. But they had left one little space for me, and Queen Salote motioned for me to come and sit down beside her.

As I shook hands with her for the first time, I immediately felt her deep sincerity and maternal solicitude, qualities I admired more and more in her as my years in her Kingdom rolled by. I knew she was interested in our Mission and was glad to be there with us.

As for me, well, I was just simply thrilled through and through. When I looked out on the "malae" (lawn) and saw what a huge crowd of people was present, I guess I felt like St. Paul must have felt in that famous Athens square, the Areopagus. Immediately and without the least hesitation, I decided to make a speech.

I whispered to Her Majesty, "May I speak?"
With a big smile, she nodded her approval.

As I watched the complicated and beautiful ceremony of royal kava-making, I began to wonder just **when** I should speak, for I knew there must be a special time for that. I was beginning to be sorry I had made this rash request. It would be embarrassing to address the people in such circumstances and with absolutely no preparation.

But I turned again to the Queen and said, "Pardon my ignorance of Tongan etiquette. When should I start my speech?"

She whispered reassuringly, "Don't worry, Patele. I'll let you know."

A little later the master of ceremonies announced in a thunderous voice that the kava was ready to serve, and Queen Salote whispered to me, "Now is the time."

As I arose, I sensed a shock of surprise and indignation sweeping through the throng, and suddenly it dawned on me that I had made a faux pas. One must never stand to speak in the presence of Her Majesty! It simply isn't done at a strictly Tongan ceremony like that where everyone, even the Queen, was sitting on the ground. But it was too late. The disrespectful deed was done.

I had to think fast. There's nothing like taking the bull by the horns. So, with all outward calmness, I proceeded to explain the reason for my action.

"E Afiona (Your Majesty)," I began. "I notice a movement of indignant surprise on the faces of this august assembly. How dare I arise to speak in the presence of the Queen of Tonga? Let me hasten to explain. As a white man, according to the white man's custom I am obliged to arise and remain standing. It would not be respectful for me to do otherwise. For the same reason you must remain seated. It is your custom — your mark of respect for your gracious Queen. Please don't be angry with me. Now you understand that I stand for no other reason than to show, in the white man's way, the deepest respect and admiration for Her Majesty, Queen Salote Tupou."

Thanks to her kindly smile of approval, that little introduction worked wonders. Every face in the crowd was soon shining with peace and attention and eagerness.

"Before I give you the message that I have for you today," I continued, "allow me, first of all, to tell you a story."

Everyone settled down and relaxed. They just love stories. In that, they are no different from the rest of the world. Everyone loves stories.

"A few months ago," I told them, "I called at Honolulu, Hawaii. I had a few hours to spare, so I visited the famous Bishop Museum there, which is outstanding for its Polynesian treasures. An elderly Hawaiian woman was my guide. I spoke Tongan to her and she spoke Hawaiian to me and we understood each other very well. She knew English too.

"I visited and admired a huge hall known as the Tongan Room. Then my guide said, with deep emotion, 'Now, Father, I'm going to show you the greatest treasures in all Hawaii.' She led me into another large hall where all the royal paraphernalia of the late Queen Liliuokalani was on exhibition. There were her pearl-inlaid throne, her sceptor, her crown, and her royal cloak made like a Samoan fine mat but decorated with precious red feathers from a certain little bird which is now extinct. This royal garment is valued at a million dollars.

"My guide showed such enthusiasm, such deep veneration and devotion, that I couldn't help asking the question that had been in my mind all the time, 'What became of Queen Liliuokalani? Who is her successor?'

"The woman's voice quivered with emotion and her eyes filled with tears. 'She was deposed in 1894,' she told me. 'Then she died. We no longer have any Queen. Those happy days of old Hawaii are gone forever.'"

My audience was listening tensely now and the silence was profound. The moment was right for my rhetorical question: "Sii Kainga o Tonga monuia (dear brethren of blessed Tonga), will there ever be a time, in the future history of Tonga, when the royal robes, the throne, the sceptor and all the personal treasures of your beloved Queen, will be exhibited in a museum and visitors will be asking, as I asked in Hawaii, 'Where is your Queen?' Will someone answer sadly, 'There is no longer any Queen or any King in Tonga. Those happy days are gone forever'? Will such a time ever come, my friends?"

I paused and the silence was breathless. How they love oratory!

After an impressive moment, I shouted, "No! No! This shall never happen if you remember what I tell you now. Be faithful to your good Tongan customs and language. Be faithful to God and religion. Be faithful to your traditions.

"In Tonga you have no silver mines or gold mines, as some countries have. But you have a far more precious treasure, feo'ofoofani (brotherly love). You have that wonderful family spirit, that willingness to help each other. That is your God-given gold and silver. That is your treasure. That is why the royal coat of arms bears the words: 'Koe Otua mo Tonga ko hoku Tofia' (God and Tonga are my heritage).

"Cherish your God-given heritage. Don't lose it by a silly and servile imitation of the white man and his customs and manners. Remember, each nation has its own customs, its own traditions, its own language. Keep yours. Love them. They are part of God's plan for your happiness. Be faithful to God.

"Now I must warn you of a new 'religion' that is growing among you....."

I could sense painful surprise and eager curiosity in my listeners. But the Queen was smiling. Was she guessing what I had in mind? Was she encouraging me to say it?

"Yes, my friends," I continued, "this new religion is an enemy of the Kingdom of Tonga. Its name is Kumete Kava (the kava dish)!"

I saw dozens of heads going down like a field of golden grain bending under a sudden gust of wind — heads of some of the big chiefs bending in public acknowledgement of guilt. And how Her Majesty was enjoying it! She knew it was for their good.

"Instead of going to church on Sunday," I continued my indictment, "many of you gather and drink kava! You are enemies of the state! You are enemies of the Queen! You are hastening the day when her throne will be in a museum, when someone will say, 'We have no Queen.'"

Another short, dramatic pause allowed the words to sink into the minds where they were needed. The Queen still smiled. She chuckled with delight when I went on, "Go to church every Sunday!

Her Majesty, Queen Salote and her grandchildren

Protestants and Catholics both — go to church! And remember — the doors of the Church are always wide open to welcome everyone!"

When it was all over, Her Majesty thanked me profusely for my little speech. It had pleased her immensely. We were friends from then on, through all my years in Tonga. Her kindness to our Catholic people is one of my happiest memories. She visited Haapai a number of times after that, but I saw her only four or five times, as I would often be away on a trip when she came to Haapai.

Now one last word, an open letter as it were, to Her Majesty, Queen Salote:

E Afiona (Your Majesty), do you recall that busy day in August, 1951, when you gave me an audience in your beautiful palace in Nukualofa where I had come to say goodbye before leaving your Kingdom forever?

How kindly and patiently Your Majesty listened to me. How sincerely you thanked me for my efforts to help your people, who were my people too.

Do you remember, Your Majesty, how just before I left you suddenly arose and, in a spontaneous gesture of motherly gratitude that took me quite by surprise, you kissed me on both cheeks?

God bless your noble heart! May He spare Your Majesty for many, many years to come! May you live to see your grandchildren, the joy and hope of your life, grow up into good and loyal men and women, filled with the love of God and of Christ, Our Blessed Savior.

May the Prince of Peace ever continue His providential protection over your little Kingdom, the happiest little Kingdom in the world. May the words of Your Majesty's splendid motto remain as true in your descendants, all down through the centuries, as they are in your gracious self: GOD AND TONGA ARE MY HERITAGE!

CHAPTER 23

AKAPITO'S THANKSGIVING

THE NATIVES' SIMPLICITY and sure grasp of truth often amaze the missionary. The way they see through externals to the shining center of reality frequently puts to shame the confused reasoning of self-styled intellectuals and gives the missionary himself a thrill at the workings of grace in their humble hearts.

There was Akapito, for instance, a fine young Catholic convert who received Holy Communion every day that Mass was said in Lifuka. Sometimes, you know, there was no Mass there because the missionary went away in his boat to some of the other islands of the group, and there was no one to take his place while he was gone.

The first child of Akapito and his wife was a pretty little girl named Theresa. She had big brown sparkling eyes, full of God and heaven's purity. When she was just ten months old she became seriously ill. There was no doctor in Haapai at the time because of the depression. It was June, 1934. So all the old women in the place came in turn to try their peculiar Tongan remedies. Little Theresa got worse and worse, however, in spite of everything — weaker and weaker.

Akapito came to the missionary's house and asked to have a Mass said for the recovery of his baby. The priest did this, but God in His wisdom took the little girl home to Himself. She died on the eve of the Feast of the Sacred Heart of Jesus. The funeral took place the next morning after Mass.

Burials in Tonga aren't like those in America, you know. The priest, dressed in cassock, surplice and stole, accompanied by five barefooted altar boys, went to Akapito's house and sprinkled the tiny corpse with holy water. Then everyone went in procession to the church. After the prayers in the church, another procession was formed and everyone went on foot to the graveyard on the beach. In Tonga it would be considered almost a sacrilege to bury anyone in anything but nice white coral sand. There's always a sermon on such occasions too, because so many people are there to listen who never come to church and don't know God.

After the burial of little Theresa, and the customary sermon, the missionary returned to his home.

About two hours later the young father came to visit him. Surprisingly, Akapito was cheerful and smiling.

The missionary wondered to himself, "Why the smiles, so soon after the funeral?" He was further puzzled when Akapito said, "Patele, here's thirty cents. It's all the money we have. Could you please offer a Mass of thanksgiving to the Sacred Heart?"

"Certainly," I told him, "but why?"

"Because — because, Patele," he replied hesitantly, "God heard my prayers. You know how much I had wished and prayed that my little girl would grow up to be a nun? — that God would someday call her to be His very own?"

"Yes," I nodded, still wondering.

"Well, you see, Patele," Akapito continued, "it was this way. After our baby died, my wife and I went to another hut to weep while our relatives prepared little Theresa for burial." (This is always the Tongan custom.)

"When we came back," he said, "we were surprised to see her dressed just like a nun. She looked so peaceful — sleeping there, with a little smile on her face. My sister couldn't explain why she had dressed her that way. But my wife and I looked at each other and smiled too. We understood it all now. Jesus had heard us, after all. Our baby belonged to Him forever now — just the same as if she had grown up and become a nun. Patele, that's why I want you to say a Mass of thanksgiving to the Sacred Heart."

The intense joy I felt, as he spoke, was like an electric shock. Truly God hides these things from the worldly wise and reveals them to His little ones. As I accepted Akapito's precious thirty cents and watched him walk happily away, I turned toward the little mission chapel and whispered my own "Thank You, Jesus!" — and much more that could never be told in words.

CHAPTER 24

A MISSIONARY'S SIMPLER PLEASURES

FINDING A SHILLING in your pants pocket when you thought you were dead broke... The smell of Boston baked beans for supper... Putting your finger on the flea and putting the flea on the spot, between your two thumb nails... Watching your pet hen march out from under the house with her brood of new-hatched chicks... The smell of pine wood shavings... The sound of a sharp saw ... The feel on the keen edge of a tool... The smell of good tobacco...

A large bowl of clean, cool kava after a long hike on a hot day... A shower after a long trip in rough seas... Sleeping in your own bed at last, after roughing it in the bush or on some back-block island for two weeks... Racing a rain shower and beating it to shelter...

When the toil of day is over and you've finished all your spiritual exercises and you sit down in your old deck chair, light your pipe and settle

Smaller pleasures of Missionary life....

down to a quiet "read" with a good book ... Sorting out your mail ... The feeling of security when the rain is machine-gunning your galvanized iron roof and you are snug and dry for the night ...

Watching two little pigs quarrel ... A kitten stalking a leaf ... Watching a bunch of brown-bellied kiddies playing "marbles" with nice round nuts they got from the bush ... The sparkle of delight when you give them candy, called "lollies" of course, all over Oceania ...

Discovering an article of yours in a magazine and wondering how in the world it ever got there ... Telling the Sisters some news they hadn't already heard ... The smell of clean linen ... A quiet "smoke talk" with some native with a Nicodemus bent who has come to you to ask and learn ... The sudden gleam of intelligence when your meaning finally dawns on him and at last he understands ... When a native brings you a nice big fish he caught, and there is no catch to the gift ...

The sound of the swish and ripple made by your boat as she glides through the water ... Fair breeze, fine sea, all sails set, native crew singing ... Then a shout from the topmast, "Land! Land!" ... Sure enough, dead ahead, a vague dark blotch on the distant horizon which means two pleasant things ... First, that the course you set ninety miles back was right and faithfully kept ... Second, that you will soon be home ...

Then the dog will bark, the cow will moo, the pigs will grunt, the hens will cackle, the roosters will crow, and the convent girls will shout, "Patele! Patele!" ... The Sisters will chuckle and make a rush for the kitchen ... While you take that long-needed shower and put on some clean linen they will prepare you a nice warm supper ... But the real reason why they are so glad and so happy? ... The Father has come back home ... And tomorrow there will be Mass again.

CHAPTER 25

SWEET-TALKING THE SHARKS

FATHER PAUL BOUSSIT, S.M., a scintillating, book-loving young Frenchman, arrived in Haapai in 1935 and was assigned as my assistant in this 12-island parish. He was eager to learn, not only the language, but also the customs and folklore of those most interesting people.

Can you imagine his reaction and the characteristic French shrug of the shoulders when I told him that the natives "call the sharks" and then catch them by putting a noose around their gills? He found it such an incredible assertion that he volunteered to go out and see for himself.

When he came back from that trip, face all sunburned and the skin peeling off his nose — came back with a whole boatload of sharks — he was so excited that he couldn't eat or sleep or take a bath or anything until he sat down and wrote the following account of his experience to his friends back home in France.

The editor of the Pacific Islands Monthly, published in Sydney, Australia, read the story with a chuckle of joy, realized he had a scoop and gave it immediate priority.

So sit down now, on a comfortable chair, and grab hold of its two arms while you listen to this translation from the original French:

"You fellows simply aren't in it when it comes to big game," Father Boussit wrote. "You may have caught some wee things, the size of your arm. But what about catching sharks six to eight feet long? Yes, siree! Perhaps the Tongans are right when they claim to be the greatest nation on earth. Tell me, what other people can lasso sharks, put a noose around their gills and yank them aboard their boat?

"Ever since I arrived in Tonga, I'd heard so many fantastic tales about shark-fishing that I was longing for a chance to investigate the matter personally. The chance came sooner than I expected.

"Grading was under way on the Mission Compound but, owing to hard times, there was a scarcity of tinned beef. You know, in Haapai the Catholic people never expect to be paid for their work on the Church or mission property. They give their labor free of charge, just as they know the missionary is doing for them. They do expect, however, that when they come to work, each one bringing his own vegetables for the noon meal, the priest will furnish the meat. According to custom he gives each man at least half a pound of corned beef. They love it too.

"But now there was no beef to be had, so the work lagged and many of the men didn't show up at all. Then the pastor got a brain wave. Why not let the "Fetuu Moana" (Star of the Deep), our homemade mission yacht, go out on a shark-fishing expedition? So I found myself aboard with ten or twelve of our shark experts, one Sunday afternoon. Shark-fishing in Tonga, you must remember, is a fine art handed down from father to son.

"The first day was a failure, as far as catching sharks was concerned, although the natives spent half the night inviting the sharks into their 'little parlor.' No spider ever sweet-talked a fly more eloquently. 'Beautiful girls of the briny deep, come away from your nice villages. Come over and bring your friends. Come over and see our new boat, a boat with a motor in it. Come over and let us see your beautiful eyes. Come aboard and we will give you a great feast. Come and let us put this sweet-scented necklace around your necks.' So it went, far into the night, but all in vain.

"The next day, however, it was a different story. No sooner had I finished my Mass than I heard the joyful shout, 'Malie! Malie!' (pronounced mah-lee-ay, with accent on the last syllable — meaning 'wonderful! wonderful!'). I rushed up on deck and sure enough, about forty feet off our port side, was a shiny fin — a terrible sight and yet a joy for our waiting eyes.

"A long pole, its end baited with a chunk of smelly pork, was held over the water. All the beautiful Tongan love language was repeated. Ah, shucks! Evidently the shark was in no hurry. I got tired of waiting and was about to go down below when the shark spied the meat. His wicked little eyes sparkled with drunken hunger. Hypnotized, as it were, and unmindful of danger, he made a dash for the meat, turned over on his back and opened his trap-like mouth, showing gleaming rows of terrifying teeth.

"The pole is drawn closer and held higher above the surface. Closer and closer comes the shark. Higher and higher out of the water he lifts his head. Now he's alongside the boat. The Big Moment has arrived. The lasso is slipped gently over his head. It slips down behind the gills. Then a swift, strong jerk! One of the stronger natives takes a huge club and brains Mr. Shark, who is then hauled aboard, promptly insulted with language that wouldn't look well in print, and then honored with a little tune played on conch shells, tin cans and pots and pans. Pandemonium let loose!

"Before dinner time, three more huge sharks were caught in the same manner and welcomed with the same ceremonies. Then we met up with a 13-foot veteran who was too smart for our side. He refused to come near enough to be lassoed. Yet, with an unexpected exhibition of lightning-like speed, he succeeded in making off with our bait.

"After capturing two more 7-footers we decided to call it a day and set sail for home. As soon as we came within a few miles of shore the deafening din of the conch-shell broadcasting began. The natives must tell the world that our expedition was a success. Of course they had to give the biggest shark to the governor, according to Tongan custom.

"Stronger and stronger, wilder and wilder, grew the chorus of conch shells. Arriving at the Mission Compound, we were greeted with smiles and more smiles — and a nice big bowl of cooling kava. Then with many gestures and much Tongan humor, the bare outlines of the broadcast were filled in with details and dramatized comments. And, to top it all off, it seems I am to be remembered in history as the missionary who catches sharks.

"The next day the whole population of the town of Lifuka came to offer their services. It was a scorching hot day, but my! how they labored! What strength in their arms! What joyful peals of laughter rang through the air as the work of leveling the Mission Compound proceeded! Why? Because over there, across the way, beneath a smoldering mound (the Tongan 'fireless cooker'), hundreds and hundreds of pounds of shark meat and native vegetables were baking brown and crisp. The mere thought of all that food was enough to make every man of them work.

"So there you are, folks. Come down to Tonga some time and 'the missionary who catches sharks' will show you how he does it."

* * *

WHEN I LEFT Tonga in 1951, Father Boussit was 51 years old and in charge of the Cathedral parish of the quaint village of Maufanga, not far from the bright little town of Nukualofa, capital of the Kingdom. If you ever go to Tonga (and I hope you do), go to Maufanga and ask him, "Are you the missionary who catches sharks?" Watch him smile and turn instinctively toward the north, toward Haapai, a hundred miles away. See how his eyes sparkle with memories, as he recalls that famous shark-fishing expedition when he saw with his own eyes that they really call the sharks and sweet-talk them and slip a noose around their slimy gills.

"Yes, siree!" he'll say. "I was like the doubting Thomas. I had to see to believe."

CHAPTER 26

SOMETHING SPECIAL FOR MOTHER

YES, I MADE three trips home to Boston during my thirty years in Tonga.

Yes, God did something very special for my Mother, something never heard of before in the history of the Marist missions in the South Seas. But then, she had done something very special for God — many very special things really — during her lifetime. She was one of those ideal Catholic mothers. You know the kind. And God is never outdone in generosity.

I seldom tell the stories of my three trips home, but I'll tell you about them now because you've been so interested in all my other stories.

The first was in 1931, when I made my second novitiate at Staten Island, N. Y. The second was in 1937, a trip I like to think was specially arranged by God because He remembered how generous my Mother had always been with Him. My third visit was in 1947, when I was allowed to return to Tonga by way of the United States after attending the General Chapter of the Society of Mary in Rome. And then, as you know, in 1951 I came home for good.

Perhaps you know that, as soon as possible after a Marist has been a priest ten years, or after he has reached his 35th birthday, he is required to spend a few months in "second novitiate," to try to recapture some of the solitude and silence, the hiddenness from the world, the aloneness with God, that are his vocation as a Marist, yet can so easily grow dim when he must live "in the world but not of it" and fulfill the pressing duties of the active ministry.

So, in 1931, Divine Providence kindly arranged that Father Joseph Diehl, S.M., my life-long friend and fellow missionary, and I should both be called from our respective vicariates in Oceania to make our second novitiate, together with several other American Marists, at our beautiful, secluded Staten Island house, where every young candidate for the Marist priesthood in America spends one quiet year before he is professed in the Society of Mary.

We were there six months and returned to our mission posts, Father Diehl in Samoa and I in Tonga, spiritually refreshed and strengthened. But all was not solemn and silent at Staten Island. We had our hilarious moments too. Students of history will be astounded to learn, for instance, that the quiet, dignified place was once captured by the Polynesians that year.

The only reason why this amazing information escaped being scooped into screaming front-page headlines, and so remained unknown to the general public, is of course that it was a "military secret."

Here's how it came about. Some of those second novices (and we had some extraordinary characters that year!) learned that Father Deihl had with him a large trunk full of Samoan curios — mats and baskets, hula skirts and fans, war clubs and spears, kava bowls and tapa cloth, and many other things.

Then it happened! The brain wave! The desire for conquest and adventure! A flat-bottomed boat happened to be lying at anchor near our shore front in Prince's Bay. Someone cried, "Let's stage the conquest of Staten Island by the Polynesians!" Father Deihl was jubilant, and no wonder! Photography was one of his hobbies and this event was a photographer's dream come true. How his camera did click!

To see those erstwhile sedate and grave clergymen dressed up in hula skirts, mats, and tapa cloth, inverted baskets of gaudy colored straw on their partially bald heads; to see them savagely gesticulating with spears and war clubs, furiously attacking the invisible foe of the beachhead; to see General Phil Hasson (otherwise known as Father Hasson, S.M.,) impersonating for the moment the King of Polynesia, a black hula skirt hanging from his chin like a tremendous beard, an inverted straw basket on his head for a crown, a big fat cigar in his mouth, and his right arm brandishing a murderous war club — all this and much more besides was a delight to the photographer, as you can imagine.

In spite of the speed and utmost secrecy of this military operation, somehow or other the news leaked out. Some of the most amazing photographs came to the Novice Master's attention. The good man's bewildered surprise was something beyond words. But his reaction was immediate. The order of the day was: "PLEASE NOTE! NO MORE MILITARY CONQUESTS FOR THE DURATION OF THE SECOND NOVITIATE. CONQUER YOURSELVES INSTEAD."

When I returned to Tonga after my second novitiate I expected to spend the rest of my life there, to die there and be buried among my natives. But such was not God's will.

In 1937 my Mother had a shock. She was filled with grief and her first thought was to let her children know so they would pray for her. She had twelve children. Doctors were warning mothers against having so many children back in the days when Mother was young, just as they are now. But, as I've said, she was an ideal Catholic mother and very generous with God.

She was also a fervent member of the **Third Order of Mary,** that group of devout lay men and women who, since the beginning of the Society of Mary, have been affiliated with the Marist Fathers, Brothers and Sisters, forming one religious family with them and sharing in the spiritual benefits of the whole Society.

After her seventh child was born, my Mother was told, "You'll surely die if you have another baby." She prayed for light. She put her temporal affairs in order. (She was a good business woman.) And I came into the world. Mother nearly died, but God wasn't ready yet to take her Home. They had to feed me on goat's milk, I'm told. (So now you know how I got that way!)

Mother had four more children after me and she lived to be 78 years old. Among her last five children, all born after the doctor's warning, three are nuns (two Ursulines and one Franciscan), and one a Marist priest.

Could that hold the explanation to why we have such a lack of religious and priestly vocations today — because so many mothers and fathers are not generous enough with God? Could it be that He sometimes plans to call the children who are never born, because of parents' selfishness, to the closest intimacy with Him and to be apostles to the world that "sits in darkness and the shadow of death"? It's something to think about!

Well, as I was saying, Mother wanted her twelve children to pray for her when she was given a new cross to bear in 1937. She wanted my confreres to know too, so they would all pray.

When the news reached me in Lifuka, I went to Nukualofa to share it with the other priests there and to ask their prayers, as she had requested. I saw them all, His Excellency Bishop Blanc, last. He is usually considered a rather severe man but that day he revealed himself to me in a new light. I told him about Mother. He could see I felt it too.

To my surprise, he asked, "Do you want to see her before she dies?"

I was simply struck dumb. For a moment I couldn't say a word. Then I stammered, "Of course! Of course, I do! But this is such a surprise — so unexpected. What about Father Eckert? I'll go back to Haapai. We'll think about it and pray over it. I'll let you know."

Father James Eckert, S.M. was a young priest who had been sent only recently to help me in Haapai and to learn the language. When I asked him if he thought he could carry on alone for a few months, he promptly replied, "Father, you have only one Mother, you know! Go! Use the permission the Bishop has offered you!"

So I went home to Boston again, traveling by way of Fiji, Hawaii and San Francisco. A message had been received in San Francisco saying Mother was improving a little, so they decided to keep me there a few days to civilize me a bit. It seems I didn't look quite right. My pants had been made by an Indian tailor and my coat by a Chinaman.

When I finally arrived in Boston I found Mother feeling much better. I stayed with her several months and then one day she said to me, "God has been very good to me. Now don't wait for me to die. I don't want to keep you away from your natives too long."

Well, God liked that very much! It was her final gesture of generosity toward Him. So He arranged things so that I was still there to assist at her beautiful death, to sing her Requiem Mass and to perform the burial services. I had been given another very special privilege too, just before her death. I was allowed to say Mass three times for her in her sick room.

So that's the story you wanted to hear. May it be a little help to other mothers who give their sons to God; and to other sons whom God calls to serve Him in distant lands. "He who loves father or mother more than me," He said, "is not worthy of Me." But all the same, He more than makes up to both the mothers and the sons when they give each other up for His sake.

On my third trip home, ten years later, I traveled all the way around the world. I was one of two missionaries chosen by the Sydney Chapter of the Society of Mary as delegates to the General Chapter of the Society in Rome that year. It was the year when the Very Reverend Alcime Cyr, S.M., former Provincial of the Boston Province, was elected Superior General of the Society of Mary, the first American priest to be chosen head of the Society.

I had gone to Rome by the other side of the world, passing through the Red Sea, the Suez Canal, etc. The new Superior General gave me permission to return to Tonga by way of Boston and stop for a brief visit with my relatives and friends in New England.

Then once again I returned to my people in Lifuka, expecting never to leave them again. But you know the rest. Divine Providence had other plans for me and here I am, spending the winter of 1952-53 in the frozen stretches of Canada. As one of my confereres wrote me recently: "It's a far cry from Tonga to Canada. The good Lord would rather have obedience than sacrifice, but sometimes He knows how to send us a mixture of both. Wherever we may be, we're working for Him right along, and that's all that matters. We may be changed, but He never changes in His love and support of us."

CHAPTER 27

HE DISMANTLED A MINE WITH AN AX

ONE OF THE REASONS why it's fun being a missionary in Oceania is that you so often run into such extraordinary and humorous situations. For instance, there was the chap who came to me in our Mission workshop one morning during World War II with a big piece of what looked like green stone.

"What is it?" I asked.

"Maka afi," he replied. (Firestone, that is.)

"Firestone? Where did you get it?"

"From the reef, Patele." (Why he wanted to lie, I don't know.)

"Why do you call it firestone?"

"Because it burns, Patele. Just try it and see."

I broke off a piece with a hammer and lit it. It certainly did burn all right, with a dazzling

"Maina"

white flame and a sizzling sound. It even burned a big patch of grass underneath it — burned it black, right down to the roots.

"My, this is wonderful!" I exclaimed. "That must be a wonderful reef you have on your island. I'll have to send this information over to the United States Navy in Tongatapu."

I kept the "maka afi" and gave him a piece of Tongan tobacco in exchange and he went away happy. Then I took a larger hammer and divided the chunk into two pieces, one for my boys and one for the girls at the convent school. They all had a wonderful time that night, knocking off bits of the "firestone" and watching it burn.

Next morning another lad came around with a polished brass 2-inch pipe, about eighteen inches long and very heavy. Bits of insulated copper wire were sticking out from one of the sealed ends. It was a puzzle to guess what it was. I felt the urge to take it apart and see. But I suddenly lost that urge when the boy said, "Patele, a fellow over in Kotu Island took a mine apart the other day. This is one of the things he found inside it."

"He took a mine apart?" I cried, a sudden light flashing on in my brain. I was thinking of that "firestone."

"Yes," said the young fellow. "He took it apart with an ax."

I ran over to my bathroom where I'd hidden the "firestone," got it out and showed it to him, a big question on my face.

"Yes, Patele," he said. "That came from the mine too. He's got lots of it left."

By that time I was shouting, "Good God! Wait a minute! I've got to do something quick!"

I ran over to the convent and called to the startled Mother Superior, "Quick! Quick! Give me back that stuff your girls were playing with last night. That's TNT, Sister! TNT! The strongest kind of dynamite! It's from a live mine! A native took it apart with an ax!"

You can imagine the bewildered consternation on her face. For once she didn't say much. She just handed me what was left of the "firestone." But I could see she was doing an awful lot of thinking.

Now you just try to make a mental cartoon of the face of that poor native, who had given us this important information, when he saw me running back to him with another piece of "green stone" and heard me tell him what it was. His eyes were popping out like big glass marbles, but he clearly understood what I was asking him to do right then and there — to take my dingy and row out a mile or more off shore and drop this TNT into the deep part of the ocean.

He started off on the run, then turned around and shouted back, "Patele, what about that piece of pipe?"

"We'll see about it when you come back," I told him. "No, siree! I'm not going to take it apart. Nothing doing, my lad. The best thing you can do is hand it over to the police or to the Governor of Haapai."

"All right," he said. "I'll give it to the Governor."

Suddenly I noticed that cold sweat was pouring down the middle of my back. I was thinking of all the times we had hit that TNT with hammers. And lit it! Yet we were still alive! Those Guardian Angels of ours had certainly been on the job and working overtime!

Well, the chap who had taken the mine apart came over to our Mission Center again the next Sunday and told us his tale with all its dramatic trimmings. He and another native had gone fishing, he said, each in his outrigger canoe, near a small sandbank island.

"As we came near the island we noticed a big iron thing about four feet high. It was round like a huge ball. It had been washed ashore by the tide. We both got the same idea at once — what a fine fresh water tank it would make!" (People in Tonga drink rainwater, as no other fresh water is available.)

"We found it hard to roll it further inland. It was very, very heavy. It had a big manhole bolted on the top of it. If we could only take that big cover off, we thought, and take out whatever was inside, so it wouldn't be so heavy, then we could tow it to our island.

"Without saying a word to anyone, we went home and got an ax, and returned to our treasure island. After much hard work we succeeded in knocking off the nuts and removing the cover. The inside was all filled with electrical gadgets, wires, batteries and what not. We hadn't ever heard of a mine, so we didn't know what it was.

"We pulled and yanked and finally got everything out except the green stone lining which was about ten inches thick all around the inside of the big ball. It was tough stuff and we had to use the ax again.

"When we had about half of it cleaned out we decided to rest a while for a smoke. So we made ourselves a good big 'seluka' (Tongan tobacco wrapped in a piece of banana leaf). We were lying on our backs on the sand, a few yards away from our treasure, puffing away in sweet contentment and thinking how glad our wives would be to have such a fine new tank to drink from, when all of a sudden we heard a roaring sound coming from the inside of our tank. Then there was a great hissing noise and flames shot out from the manhole with a roar like a gigantic blow torch.

"We got so scared that we ran off to the farthest edge of the little island. Had we known what it was we surely would have jumped into our canoes and paddled away for dear life. We could see the big jet of flame shoot straight out about fifty or sixty feet, and we could feel its intense heat. Then suddenly it stopped burning.

"After waiting a while to make sure it had stopped, we came close to it and found that the intense heat had caused the metal to melt, leaving big holes in the sides. Our tank was ruined forever. It was just a pile of useless junk now. We felt so bad, Patele, to think of all that hard work we had done for nothing."

"Well, my friend," I said, "thank God you are alive to tell us this wonderful story. Do you realize that you could have been blown to bits, both of you, and the whole island too?"

"Yes, Patele," he said meekly. "I do now, since I've learned what a mine is."

"All right," I said. "Now, to show you our appreciation for what you've done to make this such an interesting day for the people of the Catholic Mission, I'm going to do as your Tongan chiefs would do. I'm going to give you a new name — MAINA (pronounced my-nah; meaning, mine). This name must remain in your family forever and be handed down from father to son.

"We shall wait for the right moment. When the kava is ready to serve, yours will be the third bowl, and in receiving it you will also receive your new name."

When the kava was made and two bowls had been served, the Master of Ceremonies cried out in a loud voice, "Ave ma a Maina." (Serve to Maina.)

With a big smile of perfect happiness on his face, the honoree clapped his hands and drank the kava down with wonderful satisfaction. He was now the first and only "Maina" in the whole Kingdom of Tonga.

To make the event still more impressive, I then rose and solemnly pinned a large medal and ribbon on his shirt and explained the meaning of this decoration. "This is to remind the world that you are Maina, the only man in the universe who ever dismantled a mine with an ax and lived to tell it."

He got so excited and so thrilled with wild enthusiasm that he jumped up and made another speech which ended with the words, "If I ever get the chance, I'll do it again!"

"Take it easy," I told him. "Don't get worked up like that. Maina, whatever you do, never, never try again to take a mine apart, with an ax or anything else! You did it once; but that was once in a million times. This means that there are nine-hundred-ninety-nine-thousand, nine-hundred-and-ninety-nine chances that you can't do it again! Do those figures impress you?"

Maina just couldn't say a word. He was too busy trying to keep his eyes from popping out of his head like bouncing tennis balls. He went happily back to his island, the big hero of the day.

A few days later the GIs came over to Haapai to dismantle another mine that had, in the meantime, been reported to them. They said to me, "Father, what's the use of us coming over here? You've got a guy who does it with an ax! But we're telling you, Father, he's one in a million!"

The Governor asked them what he should do with the "piece of brass pipe" that was in his tool box. The GIs took a look at it and were astounded to find that it was the mercury and TNT detonator from the mine.

"If that innocent looking piece of brass pipe should explode," they told the Governor, "it would blow your whole house and everybody in it into smithereens in the twinkling of an eye!"

"Please take it away," the poor man pleaded. "Take it away, quick! I don't want it any more!" (And can you blame him?)

When they had disposed of it they came back to my house, wanting to meet the chap who took care of a mine with an ax. I had to tell them he had gone back to his island. But the story of how he had been given his new name with such solemn and impressive ceremonies amused them so much that I'm sure they're laughing about it yet.

CHAPTER 28

THE CANNIBALS LAUGHED TOO

ONE GOOD FRIEND of mine actually got caught by the cannibals! But he laughed himself free. And instead of making a meal of him they made a meal for him, and everyone had a grand time together.

Father Guinard is his name. Father John Guinard, S.M. He's a big, strongly built Breton with a ruddy complexion. His jovial face is always ready to bloom forth into wholehearted smiles. He's one of the oldest missionaries in Fiji, having been there for more than fifty-five consecutive years.

Fiji is an important British colony four hundred miles west of Tonga. Its original inhabitants are of the Melanesian type, with dark skin and kinky hair, because of which they are often called fuzzy-wuzzies.

I called in there on my way back to the United States in August, 1951, and having about five weeks to wait for a boat, I decided to go around a bit. I went by bus from Suva, the capital of Fiji, to the village of Natovi, one of the most picturesque spots in Viti Levu, the main island of the Fiji Group. Natovi is a highly situated hamlet, commanding a breath-taking panorama of bays and mountains, green valleys and virgin forests.

I found Father Guinard on the veranda of the local Catholic Mission Center. He was dressed in an old pair of khaki pants and an old shirt much the worse for wear. His suspenders were made of strips of inner tube rubber from an old automobile tire.

As we shook hands, his face was all smiles and his clear blue eyes were filled with almost roguish glee. Partly retired now, on account of his age and asthmatic condition, he spends most of his time reading. His eyesight is so good that he has never worn glasses in his life.

I spent a day and a night with him. After lunch and after the midday siesta, which is a must in Oceania, I came to tell him goodbye before I started back to Suva, sixty miles away. Suva, on the south coast of Viti Levu, is the main center as well as the capital. Its harbor is not large but it is well sheltered, as it is almost circular. Standing on the main wharfs, which can accomodate any large vessel, you can look across the harbor and see in the distance the green mountains of the inland district of Namosi, once a cannibal land par excellence (if one may put it that way). Namosi, away in the remote and rugged mountains beyond Suva harbor, was the area Father Guinard evangelized in the first years of his missionary work.

On this afternoon when I last saw him, I found him enjoying his "study period." He is a methodical man and so he divides his day into regular periods of different kinds of reading. Seated on an old wicker chair, sleeves rolled up, beads of perspiration on his forehead, he was reading — guess what!

"What are you reading, Father?"

"Oh, I'm just brushing up on my theology. I'm reading my old Tanquery."

Tanquery, you know, is a Latin text book, well known to all seminarians. Here was an old missionary who was still young enough, still humble enough, and still had optimisim and courage and virtue enough to reread his old school books! Just imagine, if you can, my surprise and startled reaction. Amazing! And most embarrassing too, if you know what I mean.

Another startling thing he smilingly admitted to my horrifed dismay, was that he had recently burned his more than fifty-year-old diary. They thought he was going to die "the other day," he said, and as he was about to receive the Last Sacraments he had destroyed the precious record. Ye gods! That diary would have been worth one hundred times its weight in gold!

A jollier man you never could find anywhere in the world. He was like a mountain spring in a shaded glade, always bubbling over with merriment and laughter. And this, remember, in spite of a grave asthmatic condition which robbed him of many hours of sleep every night.

During the first ten years of his life as a missionary in Namosi, the cannibal country, the constant topic of conversation that he heard, day in and day out, was how good this part or that part of the human body tasted when prepared this way or that way.

Why did the fuzzy-wuzzies like to talk that way in his presence? Perhaps they wished to give him a gentle hint and keep him constantly on the proverbial pins and needles of apprehension. But Father Guinard didn't seem to mind it a bit. Indeed he thought it was a great joke — and he just kept on smiling. Besides being a good priest and a great lover of the Blessed Mother, he was also, at heart, a very, very brave man.

Here are two examples that will prove it. First, how he fooled the mosquitoes, the millions of mosquitoes, of Namosi's dark, dank forests. They just love new blood. You ask him how he fooled them and a merry twinkle lights up his bright blue eyes as he tells you his secret.

"Simply this," he says. "I'd stuff cotton in my ears and would go to sleep and let them eat me in peace."

Then he laughs heartily at this joke. It sounds funny to hear him tell it but, brother, it takes a brave man to do a thing like that. If you don't believe me, you just go over to Namosi or to any jungle of Oceania during the rainy season and try it.

The second illustration of his bravery is much more dramatic. Yet it is only one of hundreds of thrilling experiences in this extraordinary man's life.

"One day," says he, "I was wandering around the wild woods of Namosi. I was on horseback and so was my boy, a wiry little Fijian lad. I was carrying my rifle, as the place was alive with nice, big, wild pigeons, and also because a friendly chief had warned me never to go about without it, as the natives wanted to kill me.

"Suddenly a big fuzzy-wuzzy popped out from the thicket and signaled us to stop. Doing his best to smile and to look pleasant, in spite of the war paint his face was daubed up with, he informed us that a little further on was a house where they had prepared us a nice meal. Of course he knew we were hungry.

"My boy started to shake like a leaf. He was a native himself so he knew very well that this old cannibal was telling a lie. He was sure the whole business was an ambush, a death-trap.

" 'Father,' he pleaded in a low voice, 'don't go in that house. They want to kill and eat you.'

"I wasn't at all impressed. And I was very hungry. I was also very foolish — as I found out later. I thought this old fellow was just trying to please me, to have a good excuse to wrangle something out of me later on.

"So I said to my boy, 'Come now. Stop shaking like that. Why, the next thing you know you'll be shaking yourself off your old nag. Come now, let's have a feed and please stop imagining things.'

"So we followed the fellow and entered a large Fijian house. As usual, it was quite dark inside. After my eyes had adjusted themselves I noticed, all along the reed walls, a row of the most horrible and bloodthirsty looking cannibals you ever could imagine. They were all daubed up in war paint in the most fantastic fashion, and they were all armed with war clubs, spears and axes.

"I realized the fix we were in, and I knew the only way we could ever get out alive was to do something and do it quickly. So I started to laugh! I laughed until tears rolled down my cheeks. The cannibals were so surprised to see me act that way that their big black eyes kept getting bigger and bigger all the time. They simply hadn't expected this at all!

"When at last I stopped laughing a bit, I cried out in great merriment (yes, in their language, of course), interrupted by fits of laughter, 'Excuse me, fellows. . . . I just can't help it. . . . you see, this is about the biggest joke I've ever heard. . . . you said you wanted to give us something to eat. . . . and the only thing you've got is war clubs and spears and axes... Gee wiz, folks. . . . who ever heard of a guy eating war clubs and spears, with axes for dessert? . . . . Gee, this is funny. . . .'

"The cannibals suddenly seemed to see the joke. They started to smile and then quickly broke into an uproar of laughter, while I breathed a sigh of relief and a fervent prayer of thanks. Then while we drank some good old 'yagona' (Fijian word for kava), some of the fellows got busy and prepared some food. And did we have a wonderful 'kaikai' (meal) and a wonderful time! They didn't seem sorry a bit to have been cheated out of the meal they had planned."

That's Father Guinard's story of his encounter with the cannibals. Perhaps it was men like him that the sixteenth century monk had in mind when he wrote: "The soul of one who serves God always swims in joy and always keeps a holiday in his heart."

CHAPTER 29

THE HULA DANCER WHO BECAME A NUN

MANY FINE NATIVE GIRLS in Tonga have become nuns in the congregation of Missionary Sisters of the Society of Mary. They are the pride of the Catholic Mission of the Vicariate of Tonga.

This is the story of Sister Mary Gabriel, S.M., a little native teacher in the convent school in Nukualofa. It is the story of Kasa (Flash Light), a little hula dancer, daughter of the chief of Oua, an island twenty-eight miles from the Catholic Mission Center at Lifuka, Haapai — of how God used a boat to help her become a Catholic, and a shark to help her become a nun — and of how, in the most dramatic circumstances, she became the adopted daughter of a priest whom, to this very day, she still calls her "dear Daddy."

First of all, let's take a peep into Sister Mary Gabriel's classroom in the Nukualofa convent school, and watch her make a drawing on the blackboard. Notice how eager to learn her bright-eyed, bronze-colored, barefooted little students are. She draws a picture of a ciborium, with a Host inside and above it. She writes: "Heart of Mary" on the cup of the ciborium; "our sacrifices" on the Host; and on the stem of the ciborium "our prayers."

The children listen spellbound as she explains her drawing. A sudden gleam of understanding shines in their eyes as they grasp the meaning of her words: "When we pray and offer up sacrifices through Our Blessed Mother, it is like that — we are holding the spotless Heart of His Mother and saying to God, 'Have mercy on us because our worthless sacrifice is in the Heart of Your Immaculate Mother.'"

This actually happened in Sister Mary Gabriel's classroom, not long after I returned to the United States in 1951. She told me about it in a letter — one of the first letters I received from Tonga and one of the most treasured.

Her letter was in reply to one I had sent her from San Francisco. I had been telling a group of high school girls there about Sister Mary Gabriel, when I met two nuns who were preparing to fly to Tonga. The sisters took my letter with them and delivered it to my little friend in Nukualofa just a few days later.

Sister Mary Gabriel lost no time in replying. Her letter was written in Tongan, which is my language, too, now — I think in Tongan, even dream in Tongan.

"My dear Daddy," her letter began, "I have just this very minute read your nice letter, brought to me by the two new Sisters. Oh, how glad I was! But I could hardly keep back my tears. The wounds made by your departure were opened up again, it seemed. Really they had never healed since you went away. Oh, my; when I think that I shall never see you again — excuse, me, Daddy — I am speechless!

"When the two new Sisters came into my classroom and were introduced to me, as soon as they heard my name they cried out, 'You are Father Tremblay's daughter, aren't you?' They shook hands and greeted me warmly. Little did they know how I was struggling to hold back my tears, as they started telling me all about my Dad whom they had met in San Francisco only a few days before. But let's leave this to the Lord. He will give me all the consolation He knows I need."

Let me interrupt her letter to show you a picture of her as she writes it. She is sitting on the coral sand beach of Nukualofa Harbor. Twenty-five or thirty of her little charges are playing in the surf. Nearby is a long row of Norfolk pine trees, very straight and very tall. Behind the pines is the royal palace of Queen Salote. It is a beautiful two-story building with snow-white walls and cherry-red roof, contrasting pleasantly with the green of the large, well kept lawn and the surrounding coconut trees. The grounds are enclosed by a neat stone wall about five feet high. A soldier in smart uniform is standing guard in front of the main-gate entrance.

After making sure that her girls are all busy playing or fishing along the reef, and that none of them is going out too far, Sister Mary Gabriel takes from her pocket the letter she has just received and reads it eagerly. Then she places a writing pad on her knees and, sitting there on the coral sand, begins her reply.

She tells me bits of news: "Sister Mary Susan has been in the hospital for a week now, with pleurisy. After school I run back and forth from here to the hospital. Sister has been so good to me ever since you went away. It is too bad she is sick but I think she will be better soon." (Sister Mary Susan didn't recover from her illness, but went home to God soon afterward. She was an American girl, from Waltham, Mass.)

"Sister Mary Peter is going to leave us soon," the little nun continues. "She has just been elected assistant to Mother General. Tonga needs more Sisters. Those who come here, from all over Tongatapu, tell us that they have more work than ever, but no one ever complains.

"Thanks for the leaflet you sent, explaining the novena to the Immaculate Heart of Mary. Isn't it strange, now? This very morning, just before the Sisters came with your letter, I had been explaining to my class how to offer sacrifices and little acts of mortification through the Immaculate Heart of Mary. They all seemed to pay close attention. But to be sure that it was not too deep for their little minds and to help them understand better, I drew a picture on the blackboard...."

Here she described her drawing and her beautiful explanation. As I read it, I could see those eager little eyes intently watching her. I thanked God for the alert young minds so ready to absorb the truths of Faith, and begged Him to send more laborers to His precious Tongan harvest.

Sister Mary Gabriel's letter continued: "The Sisters brought me your letter and your novena leaflet just afterward. When they told me they had seen you a few days ago — well, their eyes were filled with tears but mine were worse. They told me to send you their love....."

You've been waiting to hear about the boat, the shark and how the little hula dancer became my adopted daughter, haven't you? The story begins many years ago, in 1938, when a group of na-

The hula dancer: Kasa

tives from Oua Island came to my house in Lifuka, Haapai. Because of the big mats they wore around their waists and the huge kava root they were carrying, I knew right away that they had come for something important.

And so they had. They had come to ask me to repair their boat, a big cutter about thirty-five feet long. Boats are such necessary things in this island kingdom. To go anywhere you must have a boat, and a good one too. This was going to be a big job.

These people were perfect strangers, but the missionary saw in their request a providential way of making new contacts that might mean much for the propagation of the Faith. So the Catholic Mission workshop agreed to repair their boat. The owners would pay for the materials but we would contribute our work for nothing, as a gesture of good will on their behalf.

Three months later, after much hard work, the boat was spic and span and as good as new. The whole island of Oua was so happy that they prepared a grand festival to celebrate the occasion. All the Catholic men from Lifuka who had done the work, all the Sisters and their convent girls, the Catholic Mission Brass Band, as well as the priest and the catechist, were invited and received a royal welcome from the people of Oua.

There were kava parties, songs and dances and a great banquet, with huge heaps of steaming yams, sweet potatoes, taros, pork, beef, goat meat, turtle, lobsters, crabs and "faikakai" (a native delicacy made of cooked breadfruit and coconut milk, with a thick, very sweet syrup made of sugar and coconut oil boiled together.)

There was distribution of "prizes" — beautiful mats, dozens and dozens of them, all hand-made of course — huge baskets of cooked food, whole cooked hogs, roasted suckling pigs, fans, tapacloth, baskets and what not.

The biggest and best of everything was piled up in front of the missionary boat-builder. All these gifts and the gay rejoicing showed how satisfied they were with the job. So, when many speeches had been made (and there were indeed some fine ones), and the priest's turn came to address them, you could have heard a flea scratch its ear, and a falling pin would have sounded almost like a crowbar. (I said, almost!)

So, in the customary flowery style of Tongan public speaking, I thanked them for their wonderful reception, their fine singing and dancing. I thanked them especially for one item of the program that had won the admiration of all — a fine Hawaiian hula dance, performed by four lovely maidens, about thirteen or fourteen years old. The dance had been charmingly and modestly done, and the best of the four little performers was Kasa, the chief's daughter. The people applauded long and heartily as I praised the young dancers.

Then I surprised them by telling them that one thing was missing, one thing that made the missionary sad, in the midst of all this rejoicing. (You have to be open and direct with those people, you know — none of the subtleties of civilization for them.) After all, I said, what could the priest do with three huge cooked hogs and this big pile of mats, beautiful though they were? He had expected something much better.

The reason he had agreed to do such a big job as repairing their boat was that he had hoped, when it was finished, someone would say, "Patele, I want to become a Catholic. I realize that your love for us is inspired by Jesus who said, 'The good tree bringeth forth good fruit.' Now I know that good tree is the Catholic Church."

There was dead silence again as I finished. Then the chief rose to his feet, sadness and humble distress written on his face.

"Patele," he said, "we are so sorry to learn that you are disappointed. Now we understand that the real reason why you repaired our boat and did such a good job was on account of our souls. Not one of us understood before, but now we do, Patele. To make up for our ignorance and to make you feel happy, do you know what I'm going to do? I'm going to give you my daughter so that she may become a Catholic. That will be a proof of our appreciation of what you have done for us all."

He turned to the little girl who was all smiles over this arrangement, for she had already made friends with the Sisters and the convent girls.

"Kasa," he said, "please come forward. From now on I am no longer your father. I give you a new father whom you will obey forever."

It was now the missionary's turn to be surprised and embarrassed.

"My, oh, my! This is wonderful!"

(What else could he say?)

"Thanks a lot! I take it all back — what I said about being disappointed. Now — nothing is missing. Your wonderful festival is a complete success. Thanks so much. God bless this island and all the people of Oua!"

There was thunderous applause and everyone was happy.

Of course the Sisters and the convent girls welcomed little Kasa with open arms. She remained in our boarding school for almost eight years, where she learned English, sewing, cooking and many other things, as well as the Catholic Faith. She was intelligent and a willing worker and she grew up to be a devout and attractive young Catholic woman.

Several young men asked to marry her, but she always said no. She definitely wanted to become a nun. To test her vocation and to give her a chance to see once again what life outside the convent was like, we decided to send her back to Oua for about a year. She was reluctant to go but, obedient to her Daddy's wishes, she consented.

While she was at home her father died, but not before she had instructed him in the Catholic Faith and baptized him. Her mother died too a few months later. According to Tongan custom then, her father's eldest sister took charge of the household. This aunt determined to make Kasa renounce her Catholic Faith and vowed to "knock all this nonsense" about becoming a nun out of the girl's head.

Auntie tried everything, but Kasa remained firm. When the going got too hard for her to bear, she smuggled a note to her Daddy, begging him to "please come quick" and take her back to the convent — which of course he did.

To prevent any violence, Sulia, the terrible aunt, was given to understand that Kasa was returning to the boarding school to get her trunk and personal belongings, and Kasa did just that. But instead of taking her possessions back to Oua, she left for the Marist Sisters' novitiate in Tongatapu. When Aunt Sulia received Kasa's letter telling her that news, a storm of fury broke loose. The little novice received in return a violent letter of abuse. Her aunt declared in no uncertain terms that Kasa was forever "MOTU" — a dreadful Tongan word meaning that she was cut off completely from her relatives and they never wanted to set eyes on her again.

This, of course, was hard. Very hard. On Sundays and holidays, when relatives of the other novices came to the parlor, no one ever came to visit Kasa. No one, that is, except her Daddy, who on rare occasions was able to make that hundred-mile trip to Nukualofa. How happy she was when he came!

She had been a novice for about a year when a tragic thing happened that changed completely and dramatically the painful attitude of Kasa's relatives. Some of them were diving for fish one day (uku sioata, they call it), off the island of Oua, wearing water goggles and carrying short spears. Suddenly a big, hungry "tenifa" (man-eating shark) darted from under a ledge and devoured one of Kasa's cousins.

In an instant the sea was red with blood and bits of human flesh were floating about. Terror-stricken, the other divers swam frantically back to land. The news of the tragedy spread quickly through the village and in a few minutes the whole population of the island was moaning and weeping with grief.

"Oiaue! Oiaue! (Oh, my! Oh, my!) What have we done to make God angry like this? Oiaue! What have we done?" the superstitious people wailed.

Then suddenly someone remembered Kasa and their anger and their bitterness toward her.

"Oiaue! That's what it is!"

"Of course it is!" everyone shouted. "How foolish we were to try to stop her from giving herself to God! What was wrong with the idea, anyhow, that we should have been so angry with her? Is it not a great honor to our island?"

Aunt Sulia suddenly became as meek as a lamb and wrote a beautiful letter to her niece, apologizing for their conduct and begging forgiveness.

"God has opened our eyes at last," she wrote. "Dear Kasa, do become a nun, by all means, and when you 'pulou' (make your religious profession) be sure to let us know in advance, so we can bring many big pigs and fine mats and make a great feast for you."

You can imagine the tears of joy the little novice shed when she received that letter. You can imagine with what haste she ran to church to thank Our Blessed Lord for His loving kindness.

*Above: Kasa and her school mates.
Below: Profession Day. Kasa or
Sister M. Gabriel is on the left.*

And when the great day came (April 28, 1950, Feast of Blessed Peter Chanel), when Kasa and three other Tongan girls were to make their profession, you can well imagine who was the happiest of them all.

When the "katoanga" (celebration day) arrived and all the families of the four new Sisters came together to rejoice, the biggest pigs, the finest mats and the most eloquent orators were all from Oua, Kasa's birthplace. Many of her relatives were there, including Aunt Sulia, dressed in her Sunday best and most edifying in her prayerful and respectful attention. It was a triumphal festival that will long be remembered and talked about at many a kava party.

After it was all over, I was enjoying a quiet little chat with Sister Mary Gabriel, and I asked her, "Kasa, I understand that you were given permission to choose your name in religion. Why did you choose Gabriel rather than any other saint's name?"

I shall never forget her answer. "Patele," she said, "when the Archangel Gabriel announced to the Blessed Virgin that she was to become the Mother of God, and when she said 'yes' and the Word became Flesh, that was the beginning of the Catholic Church, since it was the beginning of God made Man, wasn't it, Patele?"

I blinked and swallowed hard. Stunned with surprise and admiration at the workings of the Holy

Ghost in the soul of this little native girl, I stammered, "Why... yes... yes, of course."

"Well, Patele," she continued, "I wanted St. Gabriel to be my special patron, so that I may become like another Gabriel for my people in Oua and, by always trying to be a good Sister, bring the beginning of the Catholic Church to the island where I was born."

God love my little Tongan daughter whom I may never see again until heaven, and send many, many laborers to help make her dreams come true!

A MARIST PROPAGANDA NOTE:

Any further information you wish to obtain about the Marist Missions of Oceania, please write to:

    PADRI MARISTI
      Villa Santa Maria,
      Via Allessandro Poerio, 63
      Roma, Italia (8-18)
        or
    MARIST FATHERS
      27 Isabella Street
      Boston 16, Mass., U.S.A.

DAUGHTERS OF ST. PAUL,

In Massachusetts
    50 St. Paul's Avenue
    Jamaica Plain,
    Boston 30, Mass.
    172 Tremont St.,
    Boston 11, Mass.
    381 Dorchester St.
    So. Boston 27, Mass.
    325 Main St.
    Fitchburg, Mass.
In New York
    78 Fort Place,
    Staten Island 1, N.Y.
    39 Erie St.,
    Buffalo 2, N.Y.
    625 East 187th Street
    Bronx, N.Y.
In Connecticut
    202 Fairfield Ave.,
    Bridgeport, Conn.
In Ohio
    141 West Rayen Ave.,
    Youngstown 3, Ohio
In Texas
    114 East Main Plaza,
    San Antonio 5, Texas
In California
    1570 Fifth Ave.,
    San Diego 1, Calif.
In Florida
    2700 Biscayne Blvd.
    Miami 37, Florida
In Louisiana
    86 Bolton Ave.,
    Alexandria, La.
In Canada
    8885 Blvd. Lacordaire,
    St. Leonard Deport-Maurice,
    Montreal, Canada
    1063 St. Clair Ave. West,
    Toronto, Canada
In England
    29 Beauchamp Place,
    London, S.W. 3, England
In India
    Water Field Road Extension,
    Plot N. 143,
    Bandra, India
In Philippine Islands
    No. 326 Lipa City,
    Philippine Islands
In Australia
    58 Abbotsford Rd.,
    Homebush N.S.W., Australia